AWAKENING TO

SELF-KNOWLEDGE

AWAKENING TO

SELF-KNOWLEDGE

by

Berta Dandler

Shanti Sadan
London

First published 2014

www.shantisadan.org

ISBN 978-0-85424-071-5

Printed and bound by Gutenberg Press, Malta.

Such indeed is Self-Knowledge: it gives one the conviction that one is completely blessed, and it requires no other witness than the testimony of one's own experience; so what can be better than this?'

Shri Shankara

CONTENTS

PREFACE

Spiritual enlightenment is the goal of life and the culmination of our quest for lasting joy, freedom and fulfilment. Whatever we achieve in the material world, ultimate and interminable satisfaction is denied us—until we awaken to Self-knowledge.

Self-knowledge implies a new direction for the great quest—within. Our mind has the capacity for profound peace and an illumined understanding. Seekers of the past and present have dived deep into their own being and found eternal wisdom, divine knowledge, which reveals the infinitude and immortality of our true Self.

The ancient Yoga of Self-knowledge (Adhyatma Yoga), focuses on the goal and the path that leads to it, and sheds light on the highest wisdom of all religion and philosophy. The chapters in this book, including two devoted to meditation, show how all may approach and apply this great wisdom.

Originally given as public lectures by the Warden of Shanti Sadan, and published in the quarterly journal, *Self-Knowledge*, the writings have been significantly revised and expanded for this volume.

SHANTI SADAN
July 2014

1

IDEAS THAT OPEN A WAY

LET US START by considering five clear and definite ideas that will help us in our quest for a deeper and illumined understanding. A spiritual way to inner peace and freedom does exist, and once gained, it can never be lost. It is both a way out and a way in. A way out of what? A way out of the restrictions of our personality. It shows us how to rise above the stress and frustration caused by these restrictions. It is also a way in. The way of the spiritual Yoga leads us into ourselves, in order to discover something deeper, stronger, quite wonderful and totally free.

We carry this freedom with us all the time, but it is as if we had lost touch with it. This is partly because of the powerful force of outer attractions, which keeps our gaze fixed on outer things most of the time. We easily become victims of superficial and conventional ways of thinking. But new openings are always possible. Our own being has its root in the realm of peace and light. This is the real basis of our experience, even now. We can re-connect with it at any time, if we are alert and responsive, and make our own experiments with the spiritual practices. This will make it possible for us to grasp the significance of a few basic ideas that are the foundation of the inner transformation.

1. I can transform my mind into an instrument of peace, freedom and power to help

As self-conscious human beings, there is no reason why we should be slaves to the moods and tendencies that arise in our own mind. These inner forces are not, like the wind or the waves, beyond our control. We have already learned to shape our mind through education and training. There is also a higher development, which anyone can pursue. This is our spiritual development, which leads us to inner peace, freedom and conscious immortality.

The idea is: I can intervene in my inner world to give a new direction to my thoughts and feelings. I can intervene at any time—at any moment. I do not have to wait for things to calm down in order to help myself. Things may never calm down! But there is a way of influencing my mind wisely and benevolently—right now.

Meditation includes this kind of internal self-management. Quite apart from the spiritual dimension of meditation, the practice gives us insight into the real-life workings of the mind. It also strengthens our ability to supervise and direct the inner life.

One further reflection. We have used the word 'instrument' in relation to the mind. An instrument is something that we can take up and put down as and when we need it. An instrument has different parts, which we learn how to control and to adjust. It is not pleasant, for example, having a radio without volume control or a shower that is either too hot or too cold. Such instruments can be more of a nuisance than a delight to their owner. The mind itself is a kind of instrument of our higher Self. As such, the mind was never meant to be a source of bondage and frustration. At times, the mind may be subject to moods, but such moods do not touch the deeper Self. The mind may be momentarily embarrassed and the body may react accordingly. These disturbances in no way influence our true being, any more than the apparent play of changing colours on the sea's surface influences the fundamental transparency of the water.

If we study the philosophy of Yoga, we will discover that such statements as 'I am sad', 'I was sad', 'I am embarrassed', and the feeling that our whole being is involved in these emotions, are based on an incomplete understanding of our experience. We are confusing the nature of the instrument, the mind, with its owner, the true 'I' or Self. Each and every one of us has a deeper centre which transcends and is unaffected by whatever happens on the mental level. This is our spiritual centre. The essence of the spiritual Yoga is to learn to withdraw our sense of identity, our feeling of 'I am this', from all that is limited, including the mind and its moods, into this deeper spiritual centre of undisturbed peace—the pure 'I'.

3

It is this crucial fact that allows us to stand back from the mental stage and view the drama as an on-looker, not as one who is personally implicated. More than this, as our key idea suggests, we are actually in a position to change the plot. We can learn to take our stand on our spiritual nature, and from that position of inner certainty and power, view any mental scene, however absorbing or intimidating, from a higher per-spective. Not least, we can invoke a new and more worthwhile scenario, or simply create an interval of peace and quiet.

Therefore, this key idea, 'I can transform my mind into an instrument of peace, freedom and power to help', reminds us of our authority as spiritual beings, an authority we may have forgotten for the time being, but which is ever established in our deeper consciousness, and can be revived through practice.

2. The spiritual unity of all life

If matured, the idea of the spiritual unity of all life prepares us for realizing the infinitude and freedom of our being. It liberates us from many of the limiting ways of thought that cause disturbance in our mind.

It is only natural that, as we enter the arena of life, we find ourselves in situations where we are pitted against others. Nowadays, we may be spared the clash of empires, but life is full of the clashes of egos, of individuals with conflicting interests and ambitions. These tensions and conflicts can happen anywhere: at work, in the home, on the road. Most of our fears and anxieties are due to the real or imagined threats of other people, or, on a more tragic level, other races, other nations, other creeds. Some competition may be good and necessary in order to rouse us to action and inspire a spirit of industry and innovation. There is nothing like a challenge to bring out our hidden potentialities. But we lose perspective and risk delusion if we forget the underlying unity which subsists at the deepest level. Our appreciation of the spiritual unity of all life is a key to the higher wisdom.

In the *Bhagavad Gita*, the idea is illustrated by Krishna when he says: 'All beings are supported by Me as beads threaded together on one string' and 'I am the Self seated in the heart of all beings'. The vision is universal and all-embracing. The same insight is transmitted in the first verse of another ancient text, the *Isha Upanishad*: 'All this, whatever moves on the earth or does not move, should be covered with God'—that is, covered with the feeling that the divine is the true essence of everything. Meditation on this verse helps us to apprehend the underlying unity and transcend the negative feeling of envy. As the verse continues: 'Do not envy anyone's wealth' or literally: 'Do not envy, for whose is wealth?'

This vision of universality is fundamental to our

spiritual progress. But how is it put into practice? The yogic approach is to work from the inside out. First plant the idea of unity in one's own heart. Silence the thoughts of antagonism, whether to individuals or peoples. Stop classifying people according to appearances or superficial facts we know about them. Do not encourage these ideas at all. Instead, reflect on the deeper source of all life, the golden thread of unity running through the apparent diversity. When our thoughts and feelings are steeped in this idea, the spirit of unity will naturally find expression through us on the outer plane.

This is not a case of seeking uniformity—of wanting everyone to follow the same path, to wear the same colours. It is a case of looking beyond the surface, of appreciating our spiritual oneness with all, and of enjoying the rich diversity of beings, of religions, of cultural expressions, from that level of deeper insight.

What can we do to foster this vision of oneness? Let us first tutor our own heart in this unitive outlook, and then we will find that our response to others is based on our growing understanding of the deeper reality underlying all. In our conversation, particularly, we are advised not to run down individuals, nations or races, or support any conversation that does so. A wise silence can prompt people to think again, and helps more than we know. We may also decide to withdraw our presence if necessary. There is a saying: 'Put the brute to sleep in those you meet.' It may be difficult to know how to bring out the best in people, but anyone can learn how to damp down the complaining and critical spirit. This negativity in conversation often grows large through our interest and subtle encouragement. 'Putting the brute to sleep' means quietly withdrawing our active support for these negative tendencies in ourselves or in others. If we are meditating on the underlying unity, there will be a force running through us, which will serve as an influence for good wherever we are. In this way, the mind becomes an instrument of peace, freedom and power to help, whether we know it or not.

All these ideas may be well and good. But life does confront us with continual difficulties. Sometimes these challenges stimulate a reaction which goes against what we know to be the right spiritual response. So at this stage let us offer not so much a principle or an idea, but a practice.

3. The practice of tranquil endurance

The practice is to visualize the two words, Tranquil Endurance, in letters of light before us, to focus our attention on them and to sustain this attention, as far as possible, for a few minutes.

The principle behind this practice applies to the whole of life, for it is in the outer life that we often meet things that we have to endure, rather than enjoy. We may be remarkably good at enduring the inconvenience of long queues, transport delays, and so on. But often, our outer endurance may be just a matter of restraint. Inwardly we may be fuming and in a very unpeaceful state. If our endurance can be sustained in tranquillity, then it has a deep spiritual value. And this can be achieved by consciously adopting this practice of tranquil endurance.

How and when should we apply it? There is a saying: 'What we cannot cure, we must endure.' The occasions are surely countless when we find ourselves in slightly uncomfortable situations that we simply cannot change: a stuffy room—or a draughty one—where there is no hope of opening or closing the window; the irritating hiss of someone else's headphones on a long journey; a pain in the body; a traffic jam. All these are opportunities to invoke the practice of tranquil endurance.

The practice will not only help us through the situation. It will also bring many spiritual benefits. Firstly, we are deliberately suppressing the complaining spirit within us, which does not help at all, and often makes a small problem big. Secondly, we are affirming our mastery over circumstances, through applying our will in a spiritual way. Thirdly, such a practice is an indirect reminder that our innermost spirit is always tranquil, always above the flux of circumstances. In recalling this truth, we are taking our stand on our real nature. The practice of tranquil endurance is linked to the idea that there is something in us which is really unaffected by the trials and irritations of life. This leads to our fourth idea.

4. My real nature is unaffected by any change

This can be briefly expressed as: 'I am unaffected'. The sentence refers to our identity as the spirit or true Self. We have heard that our familiar sense of being just the body and mind is not based on the most penetrating analysis of our experience. There is something in us which is deeper. This is our innermost consciousness. It is that which is aware of the changing thoughts and feelings: their rise, transformation and disappearance, but is never itself caught up in these psychological changes or movements.

This innermost principle, indicated by the word 'I', is the main subject of the spiritual classics of Adhyatma Yoga. It is above time, unborn, eternal. It is the hidden support that enables the body and mind to function. But it is not localised within the body. It is universal and all-pervasive. Therefore, when we have some apprec-iation of this teaching, we will find that we can affirm, with intelligence and authority, 'Come what may, I am unaffected.'

At this point, we may argue: 'But I am affected. I

am always affected. Disappointments hurt me, insults do sting, and when I am congratulated, I am naturally pleased.' What is affected in all these cases is not the true Self but the ego: the sense of 'I' when it is identified with our body and mind. The true Self is the innermost awareness that knows from within the changes of the mind and the smiles and tears of the ego, and yet is not affected in any way. It is invulnerable, established in eternal freedom. The ego may be affected, but I am unaffected, and I am not the ego. The ego is an aspect of the mind. The mind is always changing, but that which is aware of the mind, the ultimate 'I', does not change. In this sense, 'I am unaffected'. I am unaffected by any change.

This principle will help us conquer many painful feelings connected with what is called 'taking it personally'. In its maturity, it will teach us to view our personality as a detached observer and to identify with our universal Self. And so this conviction, 'I am unaffected', has the potentiality to confer a high degree of freedom on our inner life.

The last idea which opens a way, though familiar as a popular maxim, has a real application to those following the path of self-realization.

5. God helps those who help themselves

If we accept that the divine is the true essence of

everything, it follows that spiritual aid comes from a grace emanating from the depths of our own soul. This teaching is a theme of the *Bhagavad Gita*, which declares that the inner darkness is dispelled by the Lord dwelling in our heart. But in whatever way we think of the supreme spiritual force, whether internal or external, most spiritual seekers appreciate the need for higher guidance, and accept that individual efforts, alone and unaided, will not secure the final release. Help and guidance are needed: from a spiritual teacher, from the spiritual classics, and not least, from the supreme reality within our own being that is our true Self. This help, or grace, will not just come by itself. We have to take the necessary steps, making a place in our life for meditation, and also adjusting our lifestyle if necessary.

We do want an overall solution to our problems. Everyone has a thirst for complete fulfilment, lasting achievement, the end of all fretful efforts, and final peace. No doubt many naively think that wealth, power or fame will cure the hunger of the soul. But the only cure is inner light and peace leading to liberation. These spiritual blessings will not simply manifest in us due to some divine favouritism. We have to take the first step, and go on making our sincere contribution to the inner transformation. Help and light will inevitably follow, in harmony with the higher law of our being. The divine consciousness has been compared to a great fire giving warmth and light all around. Anyone is welcome to come close to that fire and get warm. Or, we may decide to keep our distance and stay in the cold. It is not for the fire to move towards us. It is for us to move towards the fire.

To explore any one of these ideas will lead to new openings and possibilities in our inner life. We will be on a path of inner progress, leading to self-realization. The goal is not distant, for it is the awakening to the true nature of the Self. We cannot really walk towards it, as it is our own immediate consciousness and being. But we need to prepare our mind for this breakthrough in understanding. We need to foster the aspiration that feels the limitations of empirical experience and longs to transcend them. And it is through the mind that has been transformed by soaking itself in the ideas that open a way, that the nature of the Self is realized, and one knows oneself to be totally free, blissful, immortal and infinite—one with the supreme reality and source of all.

2

THE VALUE OF A SERENE MIND

MOST PEOPLE welcome the prospect of serenity, and there is a serenity which we experience whether or not we are consciously following a path of self-development. Let us for the moment call this 'surface serenity'. Surface serenity may come when we have peaceful intervals in life, when all seems well with our situation, our health, our finances. Or our serenity may be gained simply through relief from a disagreeable state or situation. It may be the end of a pain, when it feels good simply to be back to normal, or a respite from unpleasant circumstances, when, for example, our noisy neighbours take a holiday. In a wider and more sombre context, our serenity may come in the form of sheer relief after a time of political upheaval, when there is a return to relative security.

But we soon learn that all these forms of serenity are incomplete and transient. The human heart becomes aware of new limitations, and seeks to overcome them by generating new wants. Besides, the surface serenity provides no guarantee of inner peace or stability when things go seriously wrong.

It is reassuring to learn that there is a serenity which is stable, strong and deep, and can be cultivated by anyone who cares to do so. Let us call this deeper serenity 'spiritual serenity', and it is in complete contrast to the surface serenity.

A profound peace exists which is not reliant on externals. Its realization depends on awakening qualities that lie latent within our own being. This pure and constant peace has its source, not outside or above, but within. It is indicated in the meditation text:

OM. O MY MIND, FIND REST IN THAT MOST BLESSED PEACE THAT IS EVER WITHIN THEE, AND FOLLOW NOT AFTER THAT WHICH IS TRANSIENT. OM

The special quality of the inner peace is indicated by the word 'blessed'. This is not surface serenity, but something deep and fulfilling. Those who attain this deeper serenity do not rely on outer supports. When St Paul speaks of 'the peace of God that passeth all understanding', he means a peace that is so rich and deep that it transcends the range of man's normal mental faculties and reveals an inner consciousness that is independent of both matter and mind. Throughout history we find men and women of inner peace whose strength comes from what they are, not from what they possess.

The spiritual Yoga is concerned with this durable peace, which is the unfailing inner support when all else fails, because it is the foundation of our nature. But we need to uncover this dimension of our being, through pacifying the mind and turning our enquiry inwards to the source of our consciousness.

Our hunger for this deeper source of satisfaction is evident from the restlessness that results whenever we set our heart on things that pass—when we follow that which is transient. The human mind has a need for consummate experience which cannot be met by material means or intellectual eminence. Yet true fulfilment is our higher destiny, and it is achieved through awakening our sensitivity and awareness of our inner worth.

How can we acquire the deeper serenity? As in all cases where we want to achieve something really worth while, discipline and sustained efforts are necessary. In the case of self-realization, this is essentially a self-training, though based on the instructions of those who have themselves made this inner discovery. What does this training do for us? It will help us to tranquillize and eventually to transform our mind into a channel of peace and wisdom leading to the fulfilment of enlightenment.

The seed of spiritual wisdom is in everyone. We do not need to give up our basic securities in life in order to follow the way of enlightenment. Physical withdrawal from the world will not necessarily help, because the mind, with its habits, tendencies and misunderstandings, is with us all the time and will interfere with our endeavours. The process of enlightening inner change is to be started and sustained from where we stand now. It is a question of adopting new ways of thought based on peace, goodwill and the quest for enlightenment. Genuine spiritual thoughts and insights, springing from a high and impersonal source, when held in the mind, create inner changes that expand our experience and give us glimpses of the deeper serenity. But true self-training depends on following the guidance of the wise. This will ensure that we move forward on the right lines. The path poses many challenges, so most students of wisdom find guidance in the writings of the spiritually great, and eventually seek out a traditional spiritual teacher.

When we first turn to the way of higher peace, it is usually the case that what is outside seems more attractive and powerful than anything we could possibly discover within ourselves. The inner glories of our true nature are not yet apparent, while the outer attractions are all too obvious and compelling. It is as if we were surrounded by magnets—strong, attracting forces that promise joy through sense-experience, and magically produce ever new distractions which absorb our attention and interest. So a kind of demagnetising process is necessary, and this cannot be achieved all at once.

Another challenge is posed by what goes on in the mind itself, which has a life of its own, quite apart from what is happening in the outer world. Even when we are not surrounded by outer attractions, we may be thinking about them. Our mind may have a tendency to get emotionally disturbed by thinking about certain past happenings. A chance association or memory can stimulate a mood of anger or irritation. All sorts of strange and varied emotions can come into play. Such is the curious life that goes on within the private world of the mind, which is chiefly the result of long-standing inner habits that have gone unchecked and un-challenged.

Therefore, we need to be patient with our mind and not overawed by its vagaries. A new and enlightened way of thought and feeling does exist and can be cultivated. This inner development is accelerated if we are convinced that there is a higher power of peace and wisdom latent within us, and that our mind can be adjusted in order to awaken this power.

The first great gift of the spiritual Yoga is the affirmation of the essential divinity of our true nature—the 'I' that supports and illumines our mental life, yet remains free and untainted. It is the ground of our being—our true Self—and its nature is perfect peace. Through achieving a profound interior stillness, this great truth is revealed. This revelation confirms our fundamental identity as the infinite, the immortal. The experience cannot be described in words, but is indicated in the utterances of the knowers of ultimate truth. These statements serve as pointers to our higher nature. Here are two examples:

> The innermost consciousness of man is the infinite bliss without a second and the infinite bliss without a second is none other than the innermost consciousness of man. *Vakya Vritti, verse 39*

> I alone am the reality present in all creatures. I exist everywhere, the support of all, within and without, as consciousness. *Viveka-Chudamani, verse 496*

The second gift of this Yoga is its universality. Spiritual realization transcends all narrowness. It is not tied to a particular religion, nation or great person. It points to a truth that is all-embracing. It is a realization of the underlying unity of all experience—not just the brotherhood of man but the essential spiritual oneness of all that is. All living beings are fragmentary expressions of one great underlying spiritual reality. Emphasis on one's own self-interest, creed, nation, race, and the consequent fear of rivals, are based on a forgetfulness, or an ignorance, of the fundamental truth of the underlying unity. Realization of this unity comes through the deeper self-knowledge: to know that the ground of one's own being is one with the ground of all being, that there is only one without a second.

The realization of this fundamental identity banishes fear. Living beings are comparable to the countless waves rising and subsiding in the sea. If the wave meditates on its oneness with the sea, its particular form will vanish, but its essential being, as water, is indestructible and one with the entire ocean. We begin with a quest for personal understanding and fulfilment, but we progress to the transcendence of individuality and the knowledge of our identity as the Self of all.

Thirdly, the spiritual Yoga provides methods whereby this higher truth of the divinity of the Self and the universality of consciousness can be verified in our experience. One's own personal experience is the ultimate proof of the teachings of Adhyatma Yoga. What are the methods? They are based on an understanding of the higher laws of the mind. When our mind has finally become tired of seeking lasting joy in the things that pass, and when we have firmly adopted a spiritual way of life, inner changes of great significance take place in the course of time. These changes crystallize as the emergence of a higher power which emanates from our divine centre. It is through this power that more and more of higher truth will be revealed to us.

In the light of this unfoldment, we can begin to appreciate the real value of a serene mind. Inner serenity, inner peace, is the most desirable condition of the human mind. In that serenity, the deeper facets of our spiritual nature are revealed, shine forth in our intellect and become our actual experience. A serene mind is a revealing mind. It is not an end in itself, but is a bridge to the spiritual realm within, a precondition for wisdom and enlightenment.

How and when can we learn to cultivate this inner serenity? Serenity is first practised in meditation. Once matured, the deep serenity will express itself in our life of action and reaction. But first there has to be the regular recourse to deliberate concentrated effort, as when we apply ourselves to our daily meditation.

When we admire statues of meditating figures, what most attracts us are the faces, which show calmness and freedom from all effort and tension. Such repose is earned by repeated dedicated efforts made regularly over a long period of time. Meditation may sometimes be promoted as easy to perform and yielding instant results. But try serious meditation and we will find that the mind does not automatically settle down to inner peace, nor is it easy to turn our gaze from the outer world. Thoughts and feelings surge up in an endless stream, and these energies will not die down out of respect for our new interest in spiritual culture. The paradox in meditation is that we have to make efforts to reach a state which is free from all effort and tension. Therefore, serenity is nurtured in meditation, always grounded in the idea that the serenity we seek is already the true nature of the deepest level of our being.

Next, serenity is to be practised in our life of action. Serenity in action is something we appreciate anyway. If we are dealing with someone who is serene and cheerful, it creates good feelings and working conditions, and leads to better results in the long term.

These days, many people are trained to respond with calm and composure as part of their job. It is a professional technique. At hotels, for instance, one may be struck by the amazing politeness and cheerfulness of the staff—only to receive a questionnaire at the end of our stay inviting comment on staff performance. But our concern is not with such 'professional' serenity— which is all part of the surface serenity. Let us work on a deeper level. We can learn how to eliminate the cause of friction and rivalry in our human relationships, and discover a real and spontaneous harmony, through a deeper vision of the inner unity of all.

How can we put this into practice? First we shall briefly suggest active measures, and then raise something for deeper consideration. Often we talk of our day as being terribly busy and full of unpredicted hassles. But in the course of every day there are moments, minutes, perhaps longer, when the busy-ness abates and we are left with our own thoughts. Let us be alert to these times. They can be used as opportunities for inner tranquillization and spiritual recollection. For example, we can take a few deep breaths to clear the mind, calm down, and step back momentarily from the situation we are in.

There is an inner realm which is free from all disturbance. The outer situation is not everything and, seen from a more enlightened standpoint, is often revealed as superficial and not worthy of our tears and tensions. At these brief intervals, we can bring to mind our meditation text, and ponder it for a minute or two. We may also keep a notebook of inspirational sayings —something that can fit into a pocket and can be consulted whenever convenient. It is really a case of using our free time and energy as an aid to our goal-directed enquiry into the spiritual dimension of our own being. This is how we can use our mind creatively as a way to peace and a source of illumination.

The other aid to inner serenity in action goes deeper and may take us more time to assimilate. It is concerned with the level of our being we habitually take our stand on. The ground of our being is the infinite, immortal spirit or the true Self, but we naturally identify with our body and mind. We see the self as an individualised personality, and this is how we live our life. Unfortunately, it is a limited individuality, and from the spiritual standpoint, it is a source of bondage. Nor will our individuality last for ever. Like spring blossoms or autumn leaves, our lives, too, will fade and be finally withdrawn from this garden of the world. But in truth, we are much more than this limited individuality, and we have every right to take our stand on our immortal nature. This is to take our stand on what we really are in the deeper sense. Through spiritual practice, we learn how to disidentify our consciousness from its limited vehicles, the body and the mind, and realize the inner freedom. This disidentification, and our awakening to our true identification as the Self of all, is the goal of Yoga. To help us keep this goal in mind, we must remind ourselves of our higher spiritual nature, which transcends individuality.

Most of our troubles and frustrations are related to whether our ego gets what it wants. This constant sense of self-interest is the main obstacle to inner serenity in our life of action. The remedy to this false identification is to affirm and meditate on our identity with the infinite Self, the ground of all being, and to realize that a wave in the ocean has nothing to gain by individual self-assertion and nothing to lose when it subsides back into the sea.

The spiritual life attains maturity when the deeper serenity determines our reactions. This takes place when we have attained some degree of serenity in our meditation and in our life of action. Serenity in our reactions is a natural result of this training. Now the spirit of serenity infuses the whole of our life. It is there in our response to the world around us, and it is also there when we encounter the jolts and disturbances that life throws across our path.

THE VALUE OF A SERENE MIND

What is the wonderful secret of being able to stay serene when, for example, we are insulted, or when we are faced with some kind of loss? It goes back to that idea mentioned before, about being able to take our stand on that deeper level of our being—of affirming and holding to our true identity. It is always the ego, not the true Self, that reacts. The ego, for example, may squeal: 'I have never been so insulted in my life.' But the true Self is not affected by this disturbance. The ego may feel deeply hurt or reduced by life's deprivations —the loss of a job, a reputation, money, and not least, the loss of a loved one. These certainly can cause deep anguish. But nothing, however seemingly intimidating or crushing, can mar the fundamental serenity of our innermost spiritual nature. Serenity in reaction springs from taking our stand on what we really are—the deathless, ever peaceful true Self.

Let us end with a picture. It is a wall relief exhibited in the Victoria and Albert Museum. Here we see a representation of the death of the Buddha and the reaction of his close disciples, who are seated on the ground before his bed. Four of them are moved with grief, and their expression and posture show sorrow and anguish. But if we look to the right, we see that one disciple remains serene and strong. His mind is withdrawn from the outer scene. His response is based on a deeper understanding that has taken root: that this world is a realm of changing appearances, where

24

nothing, however dear, can be held forever. Yet there is also a realm of eternal peace, which is to be found by quietening the mental activities and turning within. In terms of Adhyatma Yoga, it is a recognition that whatever happens in the outer realm, 'My mind rests in contemplation of the ever-shining light in my soul. That light am I.' The spiritual Yoga is one of the great paths that lead to the full uncovering of man's true Self, or true 'I'—the perfectly serene state and the culmination of happiness.

The Death of the Buddha (detail)
© Victoria and Albert Museum, London

3

THE PRACTICE OF MEDITATION (1)

MEDITATION is progressive. It begins with exertion, becomes a source of peace and inspiration, and ends in self-transcendence. Like a journey that starts with a single resolute step, the first stage in meditation is to establish the practice as a habit, a regular part of our daily routine, if possible the first undertaking of the day. Its initial claim on our time is modest—yet in that crucial half hour, we learn to sit still, restrain the senses as their master, and calm and focus our thoughts. If we persevere, and are ready for it, we are rewarded with an inner peace which cannot be generated by effort, yet never manifests unless earnest efforts and deep interest have been sustained. Transcendence, the goal of meditation, means the realization of the infinitude of our true Self as the sole and absolute reality.

This deeper spiritual reality or essence underlies our personality. Its nature is peace, power, light, fulfilment, and it is the great power that makes experience possible. Meditation helps us to re-connect and merge with this divine source of our being.

Thus meditation has a spiritual purpose and is best approached in an attitude of reverence and receptivity. We feel that we are in the presence of a deeper reality within and around us, which is the source of all life and consciousness. Sitting for a minute or two in inner communion, we mentally bow to this invisible power.

After this it is suggested that we do a breathing practice.

> Focus your attention on the navel. Take a deep breath in relaxation. As you breathe in, imagine that you are drawing the breath up from the navel to the spot between the eyebrows. Hold the attention at this point for a second or two, and then slowly release the breath. Take 21 breaths in this way.

Sit comfortably on your chair or cushion, upright and centred. It is important that the central part of the body is not constricted in any way, so that our posture helps the free flow of the breathing. Once the body is poised and balanced, it can be forgotten, and this is the real purpose of establishing a good meditation posture. Focusing our attention in this way, our pacified mind will be open to the influence of the light and peace radiating from the depth of our being. Let us do this practice, allowing about four minutes to cover the 21 breaths.

Next we engage our mind in a visualization.

> Imagine that the morning sun is shining in the 'heart centre'. We fix our thought on this point, called the centre of vitality, and visualize the morning sun radiating there, and let its rays of peace, power and plenty issue forth.

After the breathing practice, which creates, as it were, some inner space, the way is open for the light from the inner spiritual sun to shine through. In our visualization practice, we keep our awareness in this central region of our body, called the heart centre, and focus on the image of a radiant sun which fills us with peace and light. It is a symbol of the self-illumined reality, which is not really localised in any place or form—but this type of concentration helps because it points to something deeper in us that is immortal, perfect and self-effulgent. Spend five minutes in this practice.

Our meditation text takes us a stage further and indicates the universality of this inner light, first discerned at the centre of our own being.

> OM. THE LIGHT WHICH ANIMATES MY MIND
> ANIMATES THE SUN AND THE STARS ALSO.
> THAT LIGHT IS BLISS. THAT LIGHT AM I. OM

This spiritual light is the supreme source of all light, the revealer of all phenomena, inner and outer. The text signifies the limitless nature of our true Self. If meditated on with trust, it will open a path to Self-knowledge. We will come to find that our real 'I' is boundless and blissful, and is the reality in all we experience.

Take your time in assimilating the text by repeating it to yourself. When your attention is held—it can be a part of the text that engages you, or the whole text— take it a little deeper into yourself through the power of your concentration. Rest in it, knowing that it refers to your innermost essence. Whenever your mind slips away, take a deep breath, look at the text again, and try once more to hold it in focus. Devote five to seven minutes to this practice.

We end our meditation session by extending thoughts of peace and goodwill to all, without exception. We do this for a minute or two.

We often feel we should wait for ideal conditions before taking up meditation. But those ideal conditions never come. On the other hand, if we can learn to practise in spite of difficulties, we really will make progress in inner peace and strength. The highest qualities within us—truth, beauty, peace, wisdom—will unfold, enriching our own life, and flowing naturally through us for the good of all.

4

THE LIFE OF HIGHER LOVE

To live a life of spiritual and dharmic* progress, intent on expanding your limited experience of a fraction of the finite world to consciousness of infinity, perfect peace, bliss and love, is real wisdom.

Shri Dada of Aligarh

ALL HUMAN BEINGS are born with an innate need to love and to be loved. Love is one of the two most precious urges of human nature—the other being the urge to know.

Love means expansion. We do not like to have our experience confined to a fraction of the finite world. Nor are we really at home with our own finite personality as it is. Planted in our nature is the need to expand, and once we have learned how to love wisely, we can bring about this expansion of consciousness, because wise love entails the forgetfulness of our narrow self-interest. Metaphorically speaking, the feet of love are on the ground, but its head stretches into the blue of infinity.

Dharma: the principle of order and harmony in the world; the universal law of righteousness; man's moral and spiritual duty.

Love need not be restricted to human relationships. There can be love of a subject, a country, an ideal, the love of humanity at large, or the love of an artist for his art. We may rise to a love of something worthwhile for its own sake. The artist, Rodin, went so far as to take the great Christian writing, *The Imitation of Christ*, and replace the word 'God' with 'sculpture', reading: 'Ah, Lord Sculpture, Thou Holy Lover of my soul, when Thou comest into my heart, all that is within me shall rejoice.'

Why is it that human beings are pressed by this urge to love, to expand, to go beyond themselves? What is the source of this powerful drive of human nature? The source of love is an impulse or intuition that emanates from the centre of our being, just as gravity pulls us to the centre of the earth. At the centre of our being is the supreme reality, our immortal Self, and it is one with all. Ultimately, it is the all, being the substantial reality behind the fleeting appearances, the infinite existence underlying the finite forms. Love ever seeks unity, and yet this unbroken unity is the ultimate fact of our true nature, which is a non-dual eternal identity. Our urge to love is a manifestation of the urge for self-realization. Every seeker, indeed every lover, is destined to realize that the goal of our quest is our own immediate consciousness and being.

If this is so, then why is this pure and perfect love apparently denied to us? The eternal perfection of man's true Self remains unsuspected as long as our mind is ruled by desires for the things of the world. When we are turned outwards in this way, our mind is unaware of our spiritual essence. A particular set of assumptions and values takes hold of us. Following the way of the majority, we neglect the enquiry into the deeper meaning of life.

A new light will dawn when we become meditative and start asking such questions as: 'What am I? What is the purpose of life? What is this world, which seems to be so real and solid, yet is changing every moment and has no real stability?' It is then that we can detect the great clue which will unfold the mystery of life to us in the deepest sense, and, at the same time, reveal the true source and meaning of love.

'The world gave you false clues,' wrote Maulana Rumi. 'You took no notice of the Clue, but went to that which is without a clue.' The clue is that everything in the world is passing and that the enduring principle is to be discovered within us.

To undertake this inner enquiry, we need to appreciate the range and limitations of our instrument of experience, the mind. We must study how that range can be expanded and also how those limitations can be dissolved in the light of higher knowledge. Our mind at present may seem to be as slippery and ungraspable as a drop of mercury, or as restless as the wind, except perhaps when it is dealing with the concrete affairs of this material world. But this is only one phase of the mind's nature. The inner essence of the mind, the constant light and being within which it functions, is the true Self, immortal and transcendent. There is a higher way of life, based on spiritual practices and values, that leads to the realization of our identity with our spiritual Self and our complete freedom from the limitations of the mind.

Little by little, the human mind can be transformed. Its weight of material preoccupations can be lightened, once we realize that we ourselves are the managers of our mental intake. We should not feel that our mind lives a life of its own and that there is little we can do about it. If we have determination and perseverance, we can transform our mind according to the highest spiritual way of life. We have the power to lead it to peace and the revelation of the spiritual light as the true nature of everything. In the deepest sense, our goal is ever achieved and realizable at any moment, as long as we are fully prepared. Yoga is one of the great paths that prepares us for this revelation.

The spiritual power at the centre of our being is comparable to an inner sun, and is the true source of light and love. This divine Self is one with the supreme Self of the universe. At this level of our being, our divine ground, the limits of mind and matter have no relevance. Spirit transcends all limitations. As such, it is one and the same in all. Our worldly experience is one of almost infinite variety, but the spiritual vision is one of underlying unity, of oneness.

The highest expression of love is to feel at one with the object of our love. Our innermost Self is the supreme principle of love because it is the imperishable reality in all. The immediate realization, 'My Self is the Self of all', is the ultimate expression of love, as well as of knowledge.

One cannot move from a life of material pre-occupations and inward frustrations, to a life of spiritual light, love and peace, in a single step. But we can take daily steps to prepare our mind for the realiz-ation of unity, to live lovingly and widen our goodwill so that it extends to the whole of humanity and all living beings. If we live in this way, more and more of the light of our spiritual nature will be reflected in our mind. Our inner state will be pacified and the faculty of spiritual intuition will become operative.

The life of higher love is sometimes expressed in negative terms, that is, as the removal of hindrances and misunderstandings in order to reveal what is already there within us. Nothing new is needed. Our innermost Self, the spirit, is ever perfect, ever one with all. It *is* love, since it has perfect identification with the innermost essence of all that appears within our experience.

This love is all-embracing. It harmonizes the highest teachings of all religions, and reveals that they point to the same goal, spiritual illumination. Boundaries of sect or creed are transcended.

God-realization is the return to our normal nature. Any other experience or position, any other status, reduces our great being to a fraction of what it is in spirit and in truth. The bondage to limited mental states, to identification with one particular body and its fears and interests, is based on a wrong understanding of what we truly are. Perfection is already the nature of the spiritual Self. We do not have to create or implant it. But we need constant reminders of the presence of the divine perfection that is our true nature, and practices which will weaken and dissolve the power of false ideas and trends of character and conduct that keep us in slavery to limitations.

When it snows on the streets, municipal workers come and throw salt on the snow. The purpose of the salt is not positive. It is to accelerate the melting of the snow which covers the ground, and be itself dissolved in the process, so that only the ground remains.

This is like the process of infusing our mind with the spiritual teachings and practices. It is not intended to pack our mind with more information or to add new and complicated elements to our inner life. The practices are like those powerful crystals of salt, that, when applied, will melt the snow of the false ideas that cover our divine nature, and uncover the divine knowledge and love that is our source. When these practices have served their purpose, they themselves are dissolved in the growing light, so that the ground of pure consciousness is revealed.

This is the general principle behind the practice of Adhyatma Yoga. Spiritual life aims at dissolving that within us which darkens our understanding. Little by little, we free ourselves from the domination of thoughts and feelings that veil the inner perfection. Once these obstacles to a spiritual understanding have been attenuated and removed, our true nature will be self-evident. This is called the negation of spiritual ignorance—the removal of the barrier set up by the untrained mind.

The method of the spiritual Yoga is not a matter of imposing on our mind a set of borrowed ideas and standards, which we may admire, but which do not spring from our own heart. We cannot transform our mind from the outside. The way of unfoldment is to create inner calm, and to plant within ourselves a profound and unifying spiritual thought—one that is based on love, kindness, compassion, harmony, universality and truth. In the Bible, we find this expressed by St Paul:

> Finally, brethren, whatsoever things are true, whatsoever things are honorable, whatsoever things are just, whatsoever things are pure, whatsoever things are lovely, whatsoever things are of good report; if there

be any virtue, and if there be any praise, think on these things.

The same sentiments are found in the sayings of Mohammed: 'Do you love your Creator? Love your fellow creatures first.' 'The best of men is he from whom good accrues to humanity.'

What is not always recognised is that this kind of teaching, if held in the silence of our mind, goes deeper and influences our outlook and our understanding of our self. We are the true gainers from cultivating these great qualities. Our mind will be imbued with increasing clarity and purity, through which we apprehend more and more of the truth of our spiritual nature.

This connection between clarity of mind and meditation on great spiritual qualities is stated in the *Yoga Sutras* of Patanjali:

> The mind is made clear by meditation on friendliness towards the happy, compassion for the suffering, goodwill towards the virtuous and disinterest in the sinful.

There is practical wisdom in this prescription. For example, we can perhaps without difficulty be friendly to the unhappy, because we may feel we are in a position of advantage. But it may not be so easy to feel genuine warmth to those who are happy, because there could be the inner hindrance of envy. This meditation on friendliness towards the happy eliminates envy, which keeps us in duality, and paves the way for the experience of spiritual unity.

Again, the sutra, by prescribing disinterest in the sinful, warns us against sustained brooding on man's inhumanity to man, not because we do not deplore these happenings, but because we can easily find ourselves lost in thoughts of rage and sorrow. We may insist that such feelings are perfectly justified. But if we are to be masters of our inner life, if we are to discern the underlying unity of all beings, focusing on man's acts of extreme ignorance and folly steals away valuable time. It will also prevent us from deepening that subtle and serene poise of mind needed for the revelation of deeper insights.

In daily life, we adopt the way of Karma Yoga, the Yoga of action. It means offering our actions and their results, our efforts and our disappointments, to that supreme spiritual force. We take sufficient care with our duties, doing our best. As for the results, there is calm acceptance, appropriate response and no heartache. Let the tiny part (namely ourselves as individuals) surrender the fruits of its actions to the great Whole, which is intrinsically identical with our deeper Self. Dedicated action is the outer expression of the life of higher love.

What is the result of this way of life? The inner

revelation of the source of love in our own heart, through the removal of psychological obstacles.

We have recognised that the need to love is one of the two most powerful and fundamental forces in human nature, and its capacity for transformation and expansion is almost limitless. The other great force is the need to know. The ultimate object of love and the supreme object of knowledge is one and the same. It is the divine reality, and the way to its discovery is to seek it within our own being, with love.

In truth, we are already that great reality, but wrong ideas create a confused picture of what we truly are. We feel we are limited individuals, yet we also want to burst all bonds, and we know deep down that we have a right to do so. There are actually no bonds to burst, nothing to fight with. Our true Self already transcends the limitations of body, mind and the world, and is ever perfect, complete and free. Progressive living is essentially the removal of misunderstandings about the nature of our true Self.

There is a Vedantic saying:

That I am not the infinite, but infinitesimal, is the misjudgement of the ignorant. But the certitude of my infinity is the means of my absorption in the Infinite.

Our thought-world has developed on the assumption that we are nothing more than the body and the individualised mind. But we are much greater than these limitations. At any time we can make use of great thoughts that will reveal the way out of our apparent prison.

The spiritual truth is too subtle and too close to us to be grasped by the processes of thought, because it is our own immediate Self. But when we follow the path of self-development, the deeper truth will reveal itself as inevitably as the sun is revealed when the clouds are evaporated. If we ensure that our days include periods of inner stillness, charged with an affirmation pointing to our true Self, we are following the direct way to self-realization.

Behind the ever-changing mind is the spirit, perfect, taintless, ever free and the source of light and love. When the mental activity is rendered serene, our sense of identity can be withdrawn from the mind and re-established in its true base, our innermost Self.

A man galloping on horseback through a meadow cannot be expected to catch the scent of the wild flowers or hear the songs of the birds. But the fragrance is there; the birds are singing. What is necessary is to stop, dismount, sit still and wait, in calmness and alertness. It is in stillness that we gain the intuition of that deeper and most precious dimension of our being.

Texts for meditation are expressed in the present tense, not the future. They relate to the reality here and now.

OM. I AM ONE WITH THE INFINITE POWER
OF LOVE. I AM PEACE. I AM LIGHT. OM

Such a text connects our intellect to the purity and
freedom of our true being. This is the Self-knowledge
that completes the life of love.

For one who has reached this peak of understanding, the deeper love is extended to all, for all is a
perfect, unbroken continuity with one's own spiritual
nature. The response to all phenomena is based on
spiritual oneness. Our destiny is to transcend all
narrowness and limitations, and realize non-duality
through direct knowledge of ultimate truth. In the
world of appearances, it is expressed as a life of peace,
beauty, inner freedom and fulfilment; and this is the life
of higher love.

5

LIGHT FROM THE *BHAGAVAD GITA*

THE *BHAGAVAD GITA* is one of the great spiritual texts of mankind, as well as a book that gives clear instructions on how to practise, live and realize the goal of the spiritual Yoga. Such scriptures are the products of divine inspiration. As in music there are melodies that charm the mind with their heavenly delight, and yet seem curiously right and familiar, so the words of these spiritual texts have a transcendent origin, yet appeal in a mysterious way to something deep within us.

The Gita does not set out to teach mankind any new truths. Its poetical verses echo the doctrine found in earlier collections of teachings, the Upanishads. Underlying the world of changing appearances, of names, forms and actions, there is a motionless, changeless and blissful spiritual reality that is truly real, and our innermost nature is identical with that reality. But while the older teachings do not give detailed instructions on how people living an active life in the world may uncover this reality in themselves, and thus realize spiritual freedom, the Gita focuses on this practical area. It suggests several ways whereby all of us, whatever our mode of life, may learn to pacify and uplift our mind, and discover the divinity and immortality at the heart of our own being.

Some spiritual classics express eternal truths within a narrative framework that is set in a particular time and place, and sometimes linked with specific external events. The Gita to some extent shares this feature. The narrative concerns an Indian prince, named Arjuna, a military commander, who is compelled to engage in a civil war against another branch of his own family. We are to understand that this is a just war, waged against a ruthless leader set on the annihilation of those he viewed as his rivals and enemies. It was declared after numerous attempts to find a peaceful solution had failed.

But just before the battle, while seated in his chariot on a stretch of ground between the two armies, Arjuna's determination and leadership falter. He decides not to fight, chiefly because he sees that people he knows and loves are, through the force of circumstances, ranged against him, and he does not wish to fire his arrows at them.

Arjuna is not alone when this mood overpowers him. In accordance with an earlier promise of support, his charioteer is Shri Krishna, whom millions revere as an incarnation of the Lord of the universe. In this particular situation, Krishna plays the role of a friend, adviser and guru to Arjuna. He knows that it is crucial for Arjuna's spiritual progress that he does his duty as a righteous warrior and goes to battle; in other words, that he fulfils his destined role. There follows a series of short discourses given by Krishna, initially to meet this situation, but actually to expound the whole of the spiritual Yoga of Self-Knowledge. These discourses include key questions posed by Arjuna, chiefly on the theme of how to deal with life in such a way that one progresses towards the goal of spiritual enlightenment.

It quickly becomes clear that the Gita transcends any particular worldly situation. Arjuna stands for any human being in search of spiritual guidance, and the words of Krishna may be conceived as teachings emanating from the Lord Himself, in a way which rises above the limits of any religion or tradition.

The transcendental wisdom of the Gita is discernible in Krishna's first response to Arjuna's wish to withdraw from the coming battle, and to his depression at the prospect of the loss of life that will ensue. Here Krishna responds 'as if smiling'—that is, as one fully aware of a completely different way of looking at things. The statements he makes in the verses that follow show that this is indeed the case. We note that Krishna appreciates Arjuna's human-heartedness, his sensitivity and his freedom from anger or war fever, by referring to what he calls Arjuna's 'words of wisdom'. Yet there is a deeper wisdom that rises above personal human emotion altogether, and it is Arjuna's good fortune that he is now to be told something of this higher wisdom. Krishna, referring to Arjuna's sorrow and pity, declares: (2:11) 'You are grieving for those who deserve no grief, and yet you speak words of wisdom. For the living and for the dead the wise do not grieve.'

Krishna then goes on to teach the immortality of the spirit, and that this eternal spirit is the innermost Self of all. He says: (2:14) 'Never did I not exist, nor you, nor these rulers of men; and none of us will afterwards cease to exist.' Notice how even at this stage Krishna hints at the spiritual equality between his own immortal nature and that of Arjuna. He does not declare: 'As one with the Lord, my spiritual nature and immortality has a magnificent splendour and glory—and your own spirit is immortal in a somewhat lower and different sense.' He simply says: 'Never did I not exist, nor you, nor these rulers of men; and none of us will afterwards cease to exist.'

In enlarging on this spiritual dimension of being, Krishna calls it the true Self, and it is never spoken of in the plural. This Self has a universal significance. It is imperishable and is present everywhere, so that no-one or nothing can destroy it. 'Know That to be imperishable by which all this world is pervaded. None can cause the destruction of That, the Inexhaustible.' (2:17)

Here we have an echo of the Upanishadic way of expression. In the Upanishads, God, or the absolute spiritual essence, is called 'That', and by using the word 'That', void of any descriptive content, the Upanishads indicate an experience far greater than our ordinary mental range, and which cannot be adequately indicated by words. And yet Krishna keeps returning to the point that, far from being a distant ideal, this same principle is our very Self. It is the true Self present in everyone's body, not as a material or mental part, but as the very essence of being, and that being can never be influenced by such changes as death or physical injury.

Krishna sees that Arjuna is not aware of this divine presence in himself or in those he will soon be fighting; and so, for Arjuna the turmoil of battle and its potentially sorrowful results are all too real. But in this phase of Krishna's teaching, the reason why Arjuna is told not to grieve, is that from the highest spiritual standpoint, there is never anything to grieve about.

Krishna has sown seeds of the highest knowledge, and these will germinate in due time. But Krishna also knows that Arjuna is not yet ready to understand fully and take his stand on this highest teaching. He therefore urges Arjuna to fight as a sacred duty in defence of righteousness. He will also teach Arjuna how he can perform this duty without personal animosity, in inner peace, and in a spirit of devotion to God.

We notice throughout the *Bhagavad Gita* that the advice given by Krishna to Arjuna involves a change of mind and heart. This idea of inner change is central.

The Gita seeks to encourage trends of thought that will render the mind serene and sensitive to the spiritual presence that transcends individuality and personality.

The chapter on meditation focuses very much on how to deal with this inner world of thought and feeling. 'No one truly practises Yoga who has not learnt to renounce thoughts.' (6:2) This means that with practice and technique, one can learn, first, to be more sharply aware of what is going on in the mind; and then, armed with this awareness, to direct the mind's activities, and not be pulled along involuntarily by daydreams, or be sucked into whirlpools of negative emotions and moods. Finally, this control leads to the capacity to make the mind thoroughly quiescent.

The sharper awareness of our inner state first becomes evident in meditation. In the normal thinking of an untrained mind, the thoughts move here and there according to the law of association, but appear to have no ultimate purpose over and above dealing with the immediate problems that confront us in the world. In the focused thought and feeling of a spiritual aspirant, the mental energy is regarded as a precious material that can be transformed into the light of wisdom.

The Gita presents us with the radical idea that all this mental activity—if we are lost in it—hides a much richer and deeper aspect of our being. It is like a subtle and very effective veil that mars our sensitivity to something vital within ourselves. It diverts our attention from the inner light of the spirit. It makes us forgetful, or to put it another way, ignorant, of God within.

This is the reason why the Gita focuses on our inner life and how we may learn to control it and fill it with thoughts and sentiments that will themselves have a purifying and tranquillizing effect, so that the treasure of the true Self will become clear as the ultimate fact of experience. The light of wisdom is within everyone and it is the light of fulfilment, peace and immortality.

This ability to say to certain thoughts or thought currents: 'Not wanted, not wanted', and to hold our attention on that which we do want, is fundamental to the inner training of Yoga. It also has the greatest relevance for our outer life. Concentration, or controlled attention, is the key to learning or doing anything worthwhile. On the other hand, distraction prevents us from absorbing the most simple instructions. It weakens our power of appreciation and wastes precious mental energy.

This manipulation of our mental force, even in its humble beginnings, is never an end in itself. To say 'not wanted'—to 'renounce thoughts'—is one thing. But to inwardly embrace what we do want with all our heart and soul is the more intimate and fulfilling phase of this whole endeavour. What is wanted is the realization of our divine Self, located, as it were, in the region above the mind and reason, above the known

48

psychological powers. 'They say the senses are superior to the objects; the mind is superior to the senses; superior to the mind is reason or intellect; and superior to reason is He.' (3:42) 'He' is another word for the divine in us, which begins to reveal itself when the lower powers of the mind are brought to a state of tranquillity and spiritual love, called in Yoga, devotion.

Spiritual love is one of the main themes of the Gita, and its scope is all-embracing. It is wrong to regard the Gita as advocating personal devotion to the Lord in his form as Krishna in any exclusive way. The Gita's presentation of ideas about the divine refers to the ruler of the universe, and leads to a realization beyond form and idea. Krishna is the voice of this highest of powers, so to say, and he declares: 'In whatever way men approach Me, even so do I reward them.' (4:11) There is no one way, or one symbol of truth, that is exclusively recommended. The Gita is universal and its teachings can be taken up by those of any religion or of none.

One reason for the promotion of spiritual love concerns the nature of the mind itself. We have noted how the untrained mind moves from thought to thought in a seemingly random manner, yet its movements do follow a law of association. The outer stimuli are associated with impressions stored in our memory, and this accounts for some of the surprising connections we make in the world within the mind. But it is also a fact that our thoughts and feelings tend to return again and again to things that have made some emotional impact on us. A great love or a great dislike is like an inner magnet that continually captures our attention, whether we wish it to do so or not. We can start to think about a person we love, or dislike, at the slightest prompt; and we know how with certain people, it is wise not to raise certain subjects, because to do so might arouse associations that would result in a mood of sorrow or anger in them.

As self-awareness develops, many come to sense that this aspect of mental life is a kind of bondage, and long for inner freedom. Yet these habitual tendencies of the mind cannot be mastered or dissolved solely through the practice of controlling thoughts. Something more fundamental is needed. All these little inner magnets of likes and dislikes, longings and fears, that continually claim our attention and disturb our peace, must be replaced with a great and mighty inner magnet that is so powerful that it can and will liberate us. This is the purpose of the spiritual love taught in the Gita.

The greatest magnet, the most compelling force of attraction, is already within us. It is the divinity of the true Self, holding within itself fulfilment, peace and completeness. This is the true nature of every person, the Self that Shri Krishna expounded at the start of his teachings to Arjuna. Although, like Arjuna, few enquirers are able to grasp the full implications of this teaching at first hearing, the Gita presents many ideas that we can reflect upon, and that will make it easier for us to realize the true Self once the inner conditions are right.

At least five chapters of the Gita are concerned with shedding light on the nature of God. In these chapters, Krishna speaks as God, using the expressions 'I' and 'Me'. First of all, it is made clear that if this divine power did not exist, nothing else would exist. All that we see, hear and are exists in a state of total dependence on the divine presence that underlies and pervades it. A verse conveying this idea is: 'There is nothing else higher than Me, O Arjuna. In Me all this is woven as clusters of gems on a string.' (7:7) This divine principle is the first cause and innermost essence of all, the hidden support of the realm of man and nature:

Know Me as the eternal seed of all beings. I am the intelligence of the intelligent, the bravery of the brave. (7:8)

I am the source of all. From Me everything evolves. Thus thinking, the wise worship Me, endowed with contemplation. (10:8)

Everything in the universe has its basis in this divine ground of being, but the divine nature may be contemplated more easily in those phenomena that manifest natural glory, splendour, beauty, purity and power. Yet the conception of God goes beyond this connection with limited forms. The essential nature of the divinity is formless and transcendent; it is not conditioned in any way by the world and what happens in the world. Ultimately the world-appearance is a divine illusion, and the only real element in it is the indwelling Lord, realized as our own higher Self.

And yet, just as Krishna is the friend of Arjuna, so too is this divine Lord the most intimate and reliable friend any human being can have. We will recognise this once we are ready to welcome such a relationship. 'On knowing Me... the great Lord of all the worlds, the Friend of all beings, he comes to peace.' (5:29)

The link with God as the Friend is not established by going to any particular place. It is always established, and the mind becomes aware of this link through learning to turn its attention in the right direction. This can be achieved in many ways, but they are all based on one fundamental gesture: to think of the Friend, remembering His presence with love and with trust. The maturity of this attitude is indicated in the following verse:

He who sees Me everywhere, and sees everything in Me, to him I vanish not, nor to Me does he vanish. (6:30)

One expression used in the Gita is 'Be My-minded'. This means that the mental energies, which before were spread over a hundred diverse interests, are now pre-occupied with the quest for divine knowledge. By using the word 'My-' in this way, the Gita links the idea of God with the idea of Self. The quest for a spiritual understanding and that for self-knowledge are increasingly seen to be the same thing. Ultimately we meet God as and in our own Self.

This quest is not confined to the life of quiet contemplation. The teachings were given on a battlefield, and this battlefield symbolizes life itself. The doing of one's duty has a deep spiritual significance. However humble our role may be in this universal epic drama, we are expected to play our part as best we can, with truthfulness and goodwill. Envying another's position, taking a busybody interest in the affairs of others and neglecting the moral demands made on ourselves, is a dangerous path. 'Better is one's own duty, though devoid of merit, than the duty of another well-performed. Better is death in one's own duty. The duty of another is productive of great danger.' (18:47)

Yet within the active life, the great link with the Friend, the Divine, is to be maintained, and this is one's highest duty. This link is vital and liberating when we consider our actions as an offering to God, doing our best and not worrying about the result. It is to live fully in the present moment, trusting the supreme, all-knowing source. Anxiety about results and the impression we are making, squanders our energy and hinders us from focusing on the demands of the moment. All anxieties, before, during and after our undertakings, can be safely handed over to the Lord, the Friend, who is a sure refuge and guide in any circumstance. This is part of the path of Karma Yoga, the Yoga of Action. It can be summed up in the verse:

> Renouncing all actions in Me, with thy thought resting on the Self, being free from hope, free from selfishness, devoid of fever, do thou fight. (3:30)

Here again we notice this coming together of the idea of God, as expressed in the word 'Me', and the idea of Self, where it says: 'with thy thought resting on the Self'. It could equally have been said, 'with your thought resting on God within'. Such a thought, in the midst of action, does not serve as a distraction. For God, or the spiritual Self, is not another thing competing for our attention. It is the basis of our own being and the basis of all things.

The later chapters of the Gita return to the theme of the identity of the true Self with God. Here the Gita focuses on our innermost consciousness, and how it knows, yet transcends, all that is limited.

We remember the verse that said: 'They say the senses are superior to the objects; the mind is superior to the senses; superior to the mind is reason or intellect; and superior to reason is He.' (3:42) What is it in us that truly knows? This knowledge aspect of our being turns out to be a much deeper and more fundamental principle than is ordinarily recognised. In chapter thirteen, the Gita compares all the elements of our being *of which we are aware* to a field that appears in front of an onlooker who is quite independent of the field.

This field that is seen by us as an onlooker is not just the outer world or our physical body. Something in us is aware of the inner stream of thoughts and feelings. These thoughts and feelings make up the ever-moving world of the mind. Nobody else can see our thoughts and feelings, but our innermost consciousness is aware of all this movement, while remaining motionless and constant. Therefore the Self is the innermost witnessing consciousness, not only of the body, but of the mind itself and all that it contains.

As witness of the field, the changeless and supremely conscious Self never itself appears within the field. In this sense, it is an eternal subject that can never be an object. At all times, it is the knower of the field, never part of the field. It is our immediate experience here and now, nearer to us, so to speak, than we are to ourselves. And this is the great clue to our transcendent nature. Like the Upanishads, the Gita teaches that this innermost witnessing consciousness, the true Self, is transcendent. Though it is the hidden support and revealer of all form and movement, whether inner or outer, it remains perfectly still, perfectly free, and is never really affected by anything that happens.

Nor is it the case that each of us is a self-contained knower, each separate from the other. Although there are many fields—many minds and bodies—the knower is one in all. Here the Lord, speaking in the first person, declares: 'Know Me as the one knower present in all the fields as their witness.' (13:2) The Gita elsewhere calls this innermost consciousness the spirit or *Purusha*, and all else is held to be matter, which has no independent reality, and is referred to as a divine illusion. This indwelling Self or Purusha transcends time and space. To uncover its presence in one's own being, and to realize our identity with it, is the highest end of life.

The Gita thus offers us a wide range of spiritual teachings to suit all seekers, and a mere fragment of its content has been discussed in these pages. It prescribes a way of action, a way of devotion and a way of higher knowledge. We may ask: 'Does the Gita include any teaching that can engage and relieve the mind at any time, not least when there is uncertainty, weakness or danger, and which also satisfies our thirst for spiritual experience?' A clear answer is given in chapter eighteen in the verse: 'Fly unto Him for refuge with all thy being, O Arjuna. By His grace shalt thou attain supreme peace and the eternal resting place.' (18:62)

This goes back to the idea that the Lord, the Divine, is the Friend of all beings. Like a true friend, He is one who is always there when we need Him, not necessarily to amend the outer circumstances, but to provide help in the form of courage, comfort, relief, inspiration and inner light.

This great text, the *Bhagavad Gita*, is a spiritual gift to mankind. Its awakening power—if we receive its message with trust and follow its lead—is indicated in a Sanskrit verse: 'How can death talk of him who has studied just a little of the *Bhagavad Gita*?'

6

SPIRITUAL GROWTH

THE PURPOSE of the Yoga of Self-knowledge is to remind us of our higher destiny and help us to realize the immortality and freedom of our true Self. All human beings are destined to evolve spiritually as we learn our lessons from experience and adjust our lives accordingly. The turning point is when this spiritual evolution becomes a conscious process. This can only happen when we understand and strive for the high goal revealed by the knowers of ultimate truth. That goal is nothing less than conscious immortality. It is the realization that our innermost consciousness is not individual but universal, and that one's Self is the Self of all. This knowledge dissolves all uncertainty about the real meaning of life and all doubts about the essential identity of our innermost Self with God. The truth of this identity manifests as clearly as the sun in a cloudless sky.

Our lack of direct knowledge of this identity is the root cause of our restlessness and frustration, and the source of our sense of unfulfilment. This 'human condition' is not final, and can be relieved and trans-cended by spiritual means. Expressed positively, there is a principle within us that must grow and expand if we are to be at peace with ourselves.

When a child is growing, its clothes need constant

replacement as they become too tight for its expanding body. When we start to grow spiritually, we become aware of a sense of inward limitation and stagnation. Many of the ideas, assumptions and opinions we have harboured so far, now seem to offer no real lead in life, and yet we feel intuitively that there is something more to be discovered about life and its meaning. This state of mind is a spiritual opportunity, a chance to open ourselves to new influences that will promote the true progress and expansion of the soul.

At such a crossroads in our life, the turning we take will not necessarily be a spiritual one. If we still imagine that the lasting solution to our problems will be achieved through some outer change, we shall continue to wrestle with circumstances and perhaps win a better situation. But sooner or later our new responsibilities will make their own demands and revive the old feeling of restriction. Even if we have the means and opportunity to arrange for ourselves a continuous stream of novel and stimulating experiences, rather like being a permanent tourist, we shall eventually be forced back into a humdrum lifestyle, confronted by the less glamorous path of duty and oppressed by the same inner unrest.

A good man used to pray persistently to be allowed to visit Paradise—just a quick visit to see what it was like. Eventually his prayer was granted. He was taken to the heavenly realm and there he found himself surrounded by gentle delights of all kinds, graceful people enjoying an atmosphere of the utmost tranquillity and contentment. Years later, when he died, he went to heaven. But this time he was immediately given some overalls to wear and also some gardening tools. He said, somewhat surprised: 'When I last came there was nothing to do. I simply enjoyed myself.' The answer came: 'Then you were here as a tourist. Now you are a resident.'

One moral of this story is that to transcend our sense of limitation is not a matter of securing an easy course in the outer life. Any pleasing situation can only be sustained by a certain amount of dedicated work.

Therefore, for our spiritual growth and the transcendence of our feeling of restriction, there has to be a way forward which does not deny or evade the normal demands of our earthly life, but must somehow be integrated with that life. The real solution is not a change of outer circumstances, but to work on the inner plane and to cultivate a spiritual frame of mind.

The first real stage of spiritual growth is the realization of our need for a better inner state. This is a major awakening in our life. It is not necessarily an insight that is entertained by the majority of people. For this discontent that we feel, assumes that the expanding principle within us has begun to pressurise our consciousness to such a degree that it cannot be ignored. When this happens we become more intensely aware of our inner life. This awareness often brings with it a feeling of disharmony and unfulfilment, as if something vital within our own nature is as yet unexpressed or unrealized.

This state of restlessness can be compared to the state of a chick that is still contained within the egg but is ready to break out and to experience a wider life beyond the restrictions of the shell. So, too, we are destined to go beyond all mental restrictions and enter a life of spiritual expansion leading to fulfilment. When we reach this point of dissatisfaction with our present experience, we begin to look around for some source that mirrors, or is in sympathy with, our own inner state. What we really need at this stage is a clear understanding of what is happening to us, the reassurance that all is well, and that this restlessness is essential to our spiritual evolution. It is a divine discontent, for our nature is fundamentally divine.

Who will we turn to? There are countless seeming remedies on offer, and we will no doubt sample several before we find one which earns our deeper consideration. But if we want true freedom, we will need to be told about the spiritual path and its goal, illumination, and what we have to do in order to progress to that end. It is only from the genuine spiritual teachings based on the insights of those who have realized the goal, that we will gain the light we need.

The next definite sign in our spiritual awakening is the eagerness which drives us to listen to spiritual teachings. Our attitude to hearing the truth about our divine nature and higher potentialities must be more of a thirst—a need—than a duty. This inner thirst is an essential ingredient of the dynamic spiritual life and without it no progress is possible.

This hunger of the soul is one of the main themes of that great spiritual classic, the *Masnavi* of Jalaluddin Rumi. In one story a man is seen rushing to the mosque in order to join in the congregational prayers and receive the Prophet's blessing. But when he sees that the people are leaving the mosque, he lets out a sigh of anguish and disappointment. Hearing this sigh, the people ask what is wrong. He replies: 'Alas, I have missed the prayers and the blessing.' Deeply impressed by his earnestness, an onlooker says: 'Please confer on me that sigh—that longing. It is worth far more than all the prayers of the congregation put together.'

Why are the spiritual teachings good to hear? They are not simply informative. They have an awakening power. If heard in the right way, they kindle the flame of recognition of our true identity and impart the means whereby we may adjust our inner life so that it may reflect more and more of the light of the spirit. They reveal to us the source of our feeling of restlessness and search. That source is the fact that our higher and spiritual Self is unrealized.

Listening seems to be an easy thing, but in fact it is a high art and requires conscious cultivation. This need for effective listening is signified by the expression used by Jesus: 'He that hath ears to hear, let him hear.' One might argue that the vast majority of people have ears to hear, unless they are physically deaf. It is true that our eardrums are sensitive to sound-waves, and so we hear. But listening is a different matter.

In Shakespeare's play, *Henry IV Part II*, the chief justice tries his best to question Sir John Falstaff about his doings. But each time Falstaff shields himself by changing the subject. In the end, the chief justice, in exasperation, tells Falstaff that he must be suffering from a disease, because, 'You hear not what I say to you.' Then Falstaff at last comes to the point, showing that it is not his hearing that is at fault, but his listening. He says: 'It is the disease of not listening, the malady of not marking, that I am troubled with.'

The same difficulties, often working unconsciously within us, can hinder our reception of the spiritual truth. One reason for this shielding ourselves is that the mind is generally in a state of high security, keen to avoid interference from new and challenging ideas. It prefers to remain in a state of continuous surface activity rather than to explore its own quieter depths. If it listens at all to spiritual teachings, it is likely to retreat sideways by instantly comparing what it hears with other ideas that seem similar, thus diluting and adulterating the input by this very process of intellectual comparison. But this subtle evasion of the implications of the words of truth has to be outgrown. On the path of wisdom, it is depth of mind that really matters, not breadth of information. The treasury of truth lies buried in the depth of our being. To unveil our real nature requires inner stillness, either the stillness of meditation or the stillness of perfect receptivity, resisting the tendency to lose ourselves in seemingly spiritual fancies, or to indulge in the habit of cross-referencing what we hear with other ideas lodged in our memory.

What is real listening? Rumi gives us a hint when he tells how the followers of Mohammed listened to him whenever he recited sections of the Quran.

At the moment of munificence, that chosen messenger would demand of us attentiveness and a hundred reverences.

'Tis as when a bird is perched on your head, and your soul trembles for fear of its flitting,

So you dare not stir from your place, lest your beautiful bird should take to the air:

You dare not breathe, you suppress a cough, lest that exquisite bird should fly away.

This is highly focused listening, intensely conscious, where the listeners do not want to miss a single word. There is also a sense that this is an opportunity for deeper understanding. Why? Because any genuine spiritual teachings transmit through the words something that is deeper than the words and bears the power of the experience that inspires the words.

What has been said seems reasonable enough to those who are already committed to a spiritual way of life. But we have active and critical minds, and are not inclined to take things on faith alone. If we are not certain of the reasons why we should adopt a particular school of thought or way of practice, it will not retain our allegiance for long. We must be intellectually convinced of its validity and not just emotionally impressed by its presentation.

In order to optimise our receptivity and our capacity to benefit from spiritual teachings, and yet also to give full scope to the mind's critical faculty, we need to train ourselves to apply the following sequence, which may be expressed in the formula: 'First the listening, then the analysis.' If, while listening, our mind starts to challenge, analyze and compare, then while this intense inner activity is happening, we may lose the thread of what is being said, gathering a few vague impressions overshadowed by a pile of prejudices and preconceived ideas. A better situation is the reverse of this: to forget our biases completely and allow our mind to receive as much as possible of the information that is being conveyed. Afterwards, reflect on the teachings, preferably in solitude. Then allow the objections and questions to be formulated by our intellect with its critical faculty. If doubts persist, we may return to the source of our information and raise questions with someone who has greater experience in this field. If there are no questions or objections, and we feel that we have been spiritually nourished, we will be ready to progress with our spiritual enquiry.

Is listening to the teachings enough to awaken us to a direct realization of the truth? For example, if we are told that our true Self is in essence identical with God, and we remember it, does this constitute spiritual illumination? The ultimate purpose of the teaching of non-duality is to awaken the realization that the Self is never really under a veil and is the only reality, self-effulgent and self-evident. But our practical experience suggests that most enquirers can only assimilate this radical doctrine indirectly to begin with, as a new idea in the mind, and not as a direct experience of reality that transcends the mind. In order to convert our familiarity with the non-dual principle into the living flame of truth, and to be liberated, something more is needed. This is spiritual practice.

Spiritual practice in Adhyatma Yoga has wide

implications and penetrates the whole of our life. It includes practices aimed at the refinement and mastery of our inner life, and also the adoption of spiritual values generally, such as patience, tranquillity, harmlessness and sincerity. During our active life and our interface with other people, there are countless opportunities to evoke these spiritual values and put them into practice. This is the way our faculty of spiritual wisdom will expand and grow, and lead us further along the path to enlightenment.

Not least, our practice should include the habit of reflecting on the spiritual teachings we have heard with a view to extract their inner meaning. Such pondering may be compared to sucking a sweet where the most intense and delightful flavour is encapsulated at the centre of the sweet, and will only burst upon our tongue after we have dissolved the surrounding layers. In the same way, spiritual doctrines, like the intrinsic divinity of man, or the changeless consciousness that is aware of our thoughts from within, or the principle that the spiritual light is reflected in a still mind—all these doctrines are subtle and profound, and will only reveal their richness if we give them our sustained and sensitive consideration.

We should approach the practices of whatever kind with a genuine longing for purity and freedom. This can be stimulated if we keep ourselves aware of the great goal towards which we are travelling. In our daily life, to recall some spiritual thought, some high verse from a spiritual classic, or to consult a notebook that records sayings that inspire us, will make all the difference to our ability to cope with the day and remain inwardly centred. Such recollection will also serve as an antidote to the stings of life.

A holy man once witnessed a fight between a snake and a mongoose. Each time the mongoose was struck by the snake, it retreated to a particular bush, lingered a moment or two, and then returned to the fray. It was discovered that the bush was a herb that proved to be an antidote to the snake's venom. In the same way, to revive the thought of our meditation text, to call on truth or God, to repeat a holy name, will bring light into the mind and effectively counter the adverse influence of circumstances or our own negative thoughts.

What is the purpose of all the spiritual practices which we undertake in this Yoga? It is to calm and tranquillize the restless activity of the mind and create an inner atmosphere of peace, harmony and clarity. This in turn is a means to the deeper development in which the light and bliss of our spiritual nature, which is ever radiating from the core of our being, may impress our mind from within and enlighten it.

When the lower activities of the mind, those concerned with worldly acquisitions, anxieties, personal ambitions and resentments, have been subdued and replaced by inner quietude, a higher part of the mind becomes operative. This part of our mind, called the *buddhi*, has direct access to the source of wisdom, if, as a channel, it is kept pure and clear. The true growth of the soul is the increasing degree of peace, purity and clarity that we bring about by our own spiritual efforts, in this higher part of our mind.

One could compare the process of training the mind to Jesus's calming of the waters. In the Bible we read how Jesus and his disciples were caught in a storm at sea. The disciples roused Jesus, who was asleep: 'And he arose, and rebuked the wind, and said unto the sea, Peace, be still. And the wind ceased, and there was a great calm.' In this illustration the water may be compared to our ever restless mind, and Jesus may be likened to our latent capacity to direct and calm the mental activities. This divine principle of authority is present in every human being.

When we perform spiritual practices with a view to uniting ourselves with our innermost divine centre, we automatically draw on the power that has its source in that centre. We shall find that it is possible to command our mind to be still. If we persevere, the mind will respond as a servant to a master on whom it depends. In the following meditation text, our potential mastery over our mental life, and the source of this mastery, is indicated.

> OM. I AM YOUR MASTER, O MY MIND. IT IS IMPERATIVE THAT YOU SHOULD OBEY ME. BE STILL. YOUR REAL HOME AND SUPPORT IS GOD WITHIN ME. OM

The Bible also relates the episode when Jesus is said to have walked on the water. This may be taken as symbolizing that same ability to rise above the restlessness of the mind, and keep the higher part of our mind dry, so to say, in spite of the disturbances in the environments, inner and outer. To extend the metaphor, we keep the higher part of our mind dry—that is, untainted by worldly associations—by exposing it to the interior Sun of the true Self, through remembering our essentially divine nature as often as we can.

We ourselves have the capacity to choose whether to promote or disregard our spiritual progress. Choice is at the heart of all spiritual endeavour. For spirituality implies having the conviction that the progress of our soul to enlightenment is the most important thing in life. We may have other interests, some voluntary, some unavoidable, due to our work or situation. But let us engage in these interests consciously and with a clear purpose. Let us now and then pause during the day and ask ourselves: 'Why am I doing this? How much of my time is it claiming? Am I doing this purposefully and creatively, with a definite end in view, or have I become distracted?' In Yoga, this alertness or self-awareness is called conscious living or goal-directed living.

We really lift the barrier to our spiritual growth when we make the supreme goal of God-realization our own personal goal. In the *Chandogya Upanishad* this is called 'framing one's purpose'. The decision to live purposefully is itself a kind of affirmation that springs from the higher part of our mind, our buddhi. Once this purpose has been adopted, our life can be organised on spiritual lines.

Such a purpose may be framed as follows: 'The supreme goal in life, spiritual illumination, is my own personal goal and I am going to work for it.' This is the conviction that will advance our spiritual growth. Once this conviction has been formulated within us, it serves as the touchstone against which the value of all other undertakings is measured. With regard to any involvement, we have the power to stand back and affirm: 'OM. I am the director of my mind. If I judge that this interest will not hinder my spiritual growth, I shall pursue it. But if I find that I have misjudged the situation, I shall instantly change track, without remorse or repentance, but with determination to complete my spiritual unfoldment with urgency and priority.' For who knows how much time will remain at our disposal?

An elderly woman came to a holy man and said: 'I have lived a life of selfishness, and now I wish to learn the way to holiness. Teach me, and accept my body, mind and wealth.' The sage remained quiet, so the woman asked: 'Have I come too late?' 'No', he replied. 'You have come in time. Whoever comes to God before he dies has come in time, though he may have been a long time in coming.'

In seeking to realize the true nature of the Self—God within—are we doing something which is abnormal or unnatural? Will such a course result in a manufactured state of consciousness that will dissipate as soon as life confronts us with a real challenge?

It was said earlier that our true home and support is God within, the spiritual realm which is the very ground of our being. What *is* unnatural is to continue living our life unconnected with our spiritual source and unable to benefit from the peace, power, light and bliss that are implicit in our deeper nature. Thus alienated from our source, we conceive desire after desire, and none of these desires has so far led us to a state of permanent contentment. The life that is driven by uncontrolled desires and passions is the truly abnormal life, and the mind that is uncontrollable is the truly abnormal mind.

There is a Chinese saying: 'The mad mind never stops; if it did, it would become enlightened.' This saying gives us a hint of the barrier created by the restless mind, and the dissolving of that barrier once the mind becomes peaceful and still.

In fact, it is a far more advanced manifestation of nature to recover the rulership of our inner world through training our mind, so that we can choose what to think about whenever we wish to do so, and for as long as we like, and, if we so decide, to make our mind void of all thoughts and rest our consciousness in our real home and support, the spiritual Self, the innermost awareness and the substratum of our being.

Self-realization is the ultimate revelation of our nature, in the light of which all else is seen as an illusion that has never tainted or limited the true Self. In the words of Shri Shankara:

This being the Self of all is the true state of the consciousness of Atman, his supreme natural state. But when one feels oneself to be other than the Self of all, even by the tip of a hair, that is nescience.

So in seeking to realize that one's own Self is the Self of all, and the sole reality of the universe, one is being true to oneself in the highest sense. To follow this path is true faith, enlightened faith, leading to direct experience of the supreme truth. From this standpoint, the apparent multiplicity of selves that we find in the universe, and the universe itself, are realized to be none other than one's own Self. This spiritual reality is the unity within and behind all the seeming multiplicity. The knower of truth has the certainty that there is but one reality and I am verily That.

7

OM—THE WORD OF POWER

HOLY NAMES, signifying the supreme reality, are like
bridges which lead the mind from worldly cares to
consciousness of the eternal. The eternal is not set apart
from the human mind. It is the unwavering spiritual
power which underlies all mental activity. Yet our life
often draws us into an increasing preoccupation with
external matters, until our spiritual roots are forgotten,
and the world confronts us as the stern and only reality.
Practices which centre on a holy name help us to
correct this process, and reawaken the more inward and
subtle part of the mind, called buddhi, which, when
purified, is the organ of spiritual experience.

The goal of spiritual experience is enlightenment—
the knowledge of ultimate truth. When truth is realized,
all else is known as an appearance only. The supreme
spirit, Brahman, the Absolute, is the ultimate support of
all appearances. It is imperishable, and the realm of
appearances is a phenomenal expression of Brahman,
a kind of divine illusion, or 'maya', in Sanskrit. It is
that very same power which enables human beings to
think, feel, move and plan—the power behind the
mind.

What is the method for uncovering truth? It is to
learn how to awaken and develop the spiritual sense
within us. This is the ultimate function of religion,

though this higher and progressive aim is often over-looked. In the words of Swami Rama Tirtha, 'Religion, when freed from narrowness and dogmatism, is essentially a mysterious process, by which the mind or intellect reaches back and loses itself in the inscrutable source, the great beyond.'

Seen in this light, religions are paths to inner discovery. They are variations of a basic quest to un-cover what Christ called the kingdom of heaven within, and what Mohammed referred to when he told his disciples: 'I am not contained in heaven or earth. But know this for certain: I am contained in the true believer's heart. How wonderful! If you seek me, search in those hearts.'

One of the gifts of religion is that it provides symbols of the deeper reality, a reality which is too close and too subtle to grasp with our mental powers. These symbols have their own special power. That power comes into operation when we learn to meditate on these symbolic forms, words or images with love and with receptivity. When this practice is established, the material of the mind is gradually transformed. The mind is transformable. This is the foundation of Yoga practice. The mind is greatly influenced and changed by what it absorbs, and especially by the emotional and intellectual atmosphere we place it in. The spiritual symbols are associated with purity, peace and higher knowledge, and one means of revealing these qualities in ourselves is whole-hearted meditation on the chosen symbol.

What are these symbols? To the Hindus, they include the forms of the incarnations of God, Krishna and Rama, incidents in their lives and the deeper meaning behind them. To the Buddhists, the figure of the Buddha, or the opened lotus flower, are symbols pointing to the inner peace of enlightenment. To a Christian, the most meaningful symbol is the Cross; meditation on the life and teachings of Jesus also has a profound influence on the mind. All these forms and symbols link the mind with what is symbolized: the realm of the imperishable, the divine spirit.

Among the great practices developed in the spiritual traditions is the repetition of a name of God. The name represents the divinity, and yet points beyond itself. Such names are Rama, Krishna, Allah, Christ, the word God, and, not least, the holy syllable OM. Repetition, performed with one-pointed concentration and love, enables our understanding to penetrate more deeply into the spiritual realm within our own being. It makes a clearing in the mind, and releases it from bondage to the material.

There is a verse by the devotional poet, Tulsidas: 'O Rama, thy holy name is father and mother to me! It is my friend, my Guru, my loving companion. It is the shining path.' The saint Shri Dada of Aligarh called repetition of the name of the Lord a sure medicine for the disease of worldliness. Such repetition can be easily established, and helps countless people bear the ups and downs of life with courage and equanimity.

In the East, the science of repetition has been developed to perfection in the form of the mantras. These are short combinations of sounds, often embodying a salutation to a particular deity, which are repeated as a central spiritual practice. In addition to the mantras of Hinduism and Buddhism, similar methods are used by the devotees of Christianity and Islam, based on the names of Jesus and Allah. Such methods help to purify the mind and shield it from unspiritual influences.

In order to help us achieve our highest purpose, liberation through self-realization, the Upanishads have provided the word of power: OM. In Adhyatma Yoga this word OM begins all traditional mantrams, prayers and texts for meditation. OM is the most potent indicator of the divine consciousness, both as the support of the universe and in pure transcendence. OM also symbolizes that divine principle which the devotee can approach in the spirit of worship.

The word OM has a profound and universal meaning which is signified in many of the Upanishads. It is also a help and support for those who have not studied its meaning in depth. OM can be repeated without a deep knowledge of the metaphysical symbolism behind it. Accept that this word expresses all that is highest and holiest, and when repeating it, there will come into operation an inner force which sets in motion the purest associations within us.

When we first hear about OM it seems to be something outside us, which we learn to apply to the mind as an aid to inner peace. But the more research we do into the meaning of OM, the more we realize that it is not external at all. It is the word of power, which corresponds to the one unchanging reality within us. OM repeated is a revealing power which penetrates the layers of the mental life, and connects us with the highest truth, when uttered with reverence and love.

The pronunciation of the word OM, accompanied by spiritual affirmations, is given the greatest significance by Swami Rama Tirtha, who used such affirmations as: 'All knowledge am I.' 'All truth am I.' 'All joy am I.' 'Fearless, fearless am I.' Each sentence begins and ends with OM, said three times: 'OM OM OM. All knowledge am I. OM OM OM.' Such is one method through which OM uplifts the mind and removes psychological impediments.

What is the meaning of OM in the context of the Upanishads? The Upanishads teach that there is an eternal consciousness which remains ever the same and is the basis of all our experience. According to the *Mandukya Upanishad*, our human experience leads us, day by day, into three very different states of being. All these states are phenomenal and are lit by the light of the eternal consciousness.

The first is called the waking state, which we enter

when awakening from sleep. It is characterised by the functioning of the external senses, which receive and respond to the stream of impressions. The waking state appears to be the dominant state for the working of human life.

But each day, this waking state comes to a complete end when we withdraw into ourselves, close the doors and windows of the senses, and let our mind drift into an altogether different realm: the realm of sleep with dreams. Here again there is experience which seems similar to that of the waking state, but our environments in dream, the feel of our body, the people we mix with, are often very different to the scenario of our waking life. In dream, we can mingle happily with long lost relatives, somehow the pains of the body in the waking state have disappeared, and the laws of time, space and causation seem curiously flexible. The main thing about the dreaming state is that the outer senses are not operative: the whole spectacle takes place internally.

Then there is a third state, the state of dreamless sleep. This is a condition where dreams come to an end and there is a total absence of mental activity. How do we know? We know in retrospect, when we wake up and feel: 'Ah, I must have slept so well, I remember nothing at all.' The Upanishads hold that dreamless sleep is a state of bliss, but such bliss is of a negative nature. It is the bliss of complete absence of the pairs of opposites, limitations and finitude. It is a kind of release and close to liberation, except that it is not a conscious experience. No one becomes liberated by going to sleep each night. This state too is brought to an end by our return to the waking state.

These three states make up the totality of empirical experience. It is clear that these states are passing and cancel each other out. Therefore, in the Vedanta analysis, they do not deserve to be called absolutely real. The vast importance of the waking state comes to a humble and humiliating end when we drift into dream. The fantastic imaginings of dream are more patently unreal, and they are completely dissolved when we wake up, or when we sink into dreamless sleep. And dreamless sleep, however sweet a condition, is rudely broken when we awaken from it, and have to take on all the duties and burdens of waking life once again.

But all the time, underlying these three states, and illumining them from within, is the eternal consciousness, our true Self. It is sometimes called the fourth, or *turiya*; though far from being one more state like the others, turiya is the witness and support of all three states. Turiya is realized as the whole of experience, the Absolute. Without this turiya, this eternal consciousness, the whole phenomenal cycle of waking, dream and dreamless sleep would have nothing to rest on. This eternal consciousness is not broken or interrupted by anything. It is this consciousness which gives us the sense of continuous identity, of being the same self, in spite of apparently losing ourselves completely in sleep and dream. This is the Self to be realized, to be un-covered, in order to be liberated from the realm of the perishable.

It is with regard to this analysis of experience that the symbology of OM shows us a path to freedom. OM covers the whole of the phenomenal realm in its three phases, and also points to the transcendent, which is the light behind all experience.

This way of analysing our experience can be shown by the visual symbol OM, with the curves, lower, middle and upper, representing, respectively, the states of waking, dreaming and dreamless sleep. Above these curves there is another which is set apart from the main form, to denote transcendence, with the point signifying infinity.

Throughout experience, whether external, internal or quiescent as in deep sleep, the divine is always present equally as the turiya, just as the higher curve and the point always accompany and dominate the lower three. Therefore OM is a visual symbol representing the whole of experience both relative and absolute, finite and infinite.

The *Mandukya Upanishad* shows how the word OM is a great sound symbol. The three states are represented by parts of the sound OM itself. Here the sound OM is depicted as having three phases. They are usually represented in English by the letters A, U and M. The sound A (pronounced as in 'path') is the characteristic sound of the waking state. It is the sound of life and response to outer stimuli. A is the first sound produced when opening the mouth. The middle sound, U (pronounced as the 'oo' in 'soon'), is attributed to the dreaming state, and to states of internal mental activity, where we are withdrawn from outer objects. The sound U is also the natural sound which comes in between the A and the M, the last part of the AUM sound. This sound M indicates the third state of dreamless sleep. Even in our ordinary experience the sound 'mmm' can indicate withdrawn satisfaction and it is a more subtle and inward sound. M is also a sound of finality, the end of all sounds, marked by the closing of the mouth. The A and U seem to sink into the M, just as waking and dream, according to this analysis, are subdued into dreamless sleep.

At the end of the utterance of OM there is a short silence. Although the voiced OM ceases, its vibration continues, so that the silence becomes meaningful, allowing our focused mind to enter into the inner meaning of the symbol.

Once a teacher was approached by a disciple, who asked: 'Please teach me the nature of Brahman, the highest reality.' The sage said nothing. The disciple repeated his question, yet the sage again kept silent. When asked a third time, he said: 'I teach, but you do not understand. Silent is that Self.' Similarly, after each OM, carefully and consciously pronounced, there is a meaningful and revealing silence, beyond word and idea, indicative of the nature of the supreme Brahman. The mind is led to this silence through the dedicated and focused repetition of OM.

The *Amritabindu Upanishad* draws attention to the soundless OM, which underlies the sound: 'By sound let a man effect Yoga.' This means, by the repetition of OM, let a man learn to still his mind and make it one-pointed. 'Then let him meditate on the soundless. Then by the realization of the soundless, the non-being is seen as being.' Here the sage signifies that the

84

spiritual reality, which in ordinary experience seems to be non-existent, is realized to be self-evident and the only truly existent principle.

It can be seen that, through its symbolism, the word OM is a key to enlightenment. This is because it contains, in symbolic form, the whole range of empirical experience and also points to the infinite spiritual background behind appearances and limitations. More precisely, the analysis of OM exposes the boundaries of empirical experience with its three states and shows that we need to search for ultimate truth beyond these transient states.

Imagine a busy market place, where there are hundreds of people absorbed in buying, selling, viewing, talking, arguing, and so on. Then imagine that suddenly there is an announcement on a loudspeaker, saying: 'Ladies and gentlemen! You are now in the waking state. Please carry on enjoying it while it lasts.' Immediately, the absoluteness of the waking state and the importance of our own waking activities, are challenged. Like a lightning flash in a night sky, the hidden boundary of our waking experience is momentarily exposed.

Suppose that in our dream state, in the middle of a dream, a similar announcement informs us: 'Just to remind you: you are dreaming.' The absoluteness of our involvement in the dream world may also be challenged, and we may even be awakened by the experience.

The states are illumined and energized by a fundamental spiritual light which pervades them, but which is itself transcendent, eternal and self-luminous. This is what is indicated by the half-circle and the point, called in Sanskrit, the *bindu*. It is this spiritual dimension of our being that has to be realized. This endeavour is helped through practice based on the symbol OM.

Ultimate freedom can be achieved because the point, the bindu, is to be discovered within us. It is the innermost Self, and the three states are experiences within our own mind. Like the loudspeaker in the market place, the holy texts remind us: 'The mind is not all. Do not be hypnotized by its promises of lasting peace and happiness. Transcend its limitations by coming into contact with its spiritual substratum, the light and power behind it.' The path of the spiritual Yoga is learning to lift our attention from the region of the three lower curves—the phenomenal world—and to focus it on the spiritual principle, the still point above the curves, the bindu. This point corresponds to the divine seed in every man. When this seed is located in inner quietude at the centre of our being, and claims our one-pointed concentration, the mind loses its boundaries, and ceases to function as a limitation on consciousness. The limitless Self stands revealed as the only reality, one without a second.

Enlightenment is not something that has to be achieved, like learning a new subject. The subject of enlightenment is our own true Self, which appears to be covered by our non-awareness of its nature. OM comes as a great gift to help us dispel this non-awareness. Repetition of OM and concentration on its meaning reduces the three states to a spiritual silence. To be fully absorbed in that silence, so that the silence becomes a magnet for our attention and concentration —this is the condition for the realization of our true nature, enlightenment.

8

OUR HIGHEST POTENTIAL

IN EACH OF US there are spiritual potentialities for inner peace and wisdom, leading to enlightenment. Adhyatma Yoga gives clear methods and guidance on how we may bring out these potentialities and realize our innate freedom and fearlessness. Our true nature *is* peace, fearlessness and bliss, and we will not be satisfied with life until we are spiritually awake. We therefore need to know about our deeper spiritual potentialities.

Our latent faculties are so far-reaching that they can only be brought out gradually and through an inner training. This training has stood the test of time, and is workable in daily life for those who are serious about it. Such people are likely to enter what is called a spiritual path. The path gives us a sense of direction and is the means of making continuous progress towards the great goal of life, enlightenment.

What is the path of progress in Yoga? It is the path from bondage to freedom, from anxiety to serenity, from insecurity to fearlessness, from darkness to light. Ultimately, it is a path leading to the knowledge that our true nature transcends all limitations and is essentially one with the Absolute.

This light of understanding is not a matter of gaining something we do not already possess. It is more like a discovery or unveiling of what we really are in our inmost nature. During our apprenticeship, so to say, we learn to cultivate those tendencies which tranquillize and harmonize the mind, and awaken its capacity to withdraw into our deeper spiritual centre. In following this way, we realize that our true helper is our own higher Self, and that the source of peace and happiness is to be found in our own heart.

Let us explore an account of this great path as it is expressed in the Zen tradition, namely the ten 'Oxherding Pictures'. There are different versions of these pictures, and we will be focusing on those painted by the Chinese master, Kuo-an (Kakuan), who lived in the twelfth century. From them we can gain valuable insights about the stages of the spiritual path and the challenge that lies before us. Though known as the Oxherding Pictures, the animal in question behaves more like a bull than a mild-mannered ox, as will soon become evident. So in common with many Zen accounts, we shall refer to it as a bull.

The Search for the Bull

The first picture shows a young man standing in the midst of a scenic Chinese landscape, and he is looking for something. He looks to one side, and we have the feeling that he has been looking in all directions for something.

The picture symbolizes the beginning of the spiritual quest, when we seriously ask ourselves: 'What is the real cause of my restlessness?' This represents a turning point in our life. What leads to this turning point is the recognition that the usual distractions in which we take refuge bring no peace of mind or lasting enrichment to our life, despite all the time and effort we put into them. Yet we have a sense that our life should be moving in a definite direction. But where and how? The answer seems to be hidden, just as in the picture the man does not know exactly what he is looking for, or what he is meant to be doing.

Then why search? Because intuitively we know there is something to be found which will bring fulfilment. Our mind is beginning to become sensitive to the deeper spiritual nature within us, and needs a new kind of growth and expansion. The fact is that we are beginning to outgrow the limitations of our present mental framework. What we are searching for in this condition is really not distant from us at all. It turns out to be our true Self. An old commentary on this picture reminds us:

> The bull has never been lost. But the herdsman turned away from himself.

Finding the Traces

In the next picture, something has caught the herdsman's attention. He has noticed a track. Now he knows in which direction to turn in order to find out more.

Translating this picture into our own situation, this sudden change can happen through the impact of some teaching that strikes us with its relevance to our present state of mind, and throws light on something deeper within us. At this crucial stage, inner decisions are being made and expressed in the form: 'I must go further into this. It's important and may lead me in the right direction.'

We welcome information that helps us to follow these traces and to make sense of our situation. Sooner or later we will become active investigators, and in due time our attention will be drawn to the radical idea that the source of peace and joy is our true Self. We shall learn that the cause of our frustration is our own mind in its unenlightened state. And we shall seek further guidance on how we can adjust our inner and outer life so that we may transcend our apparent limitations and realize true freedom.

Seeing the Bull

In this picture, there is a breakthrough. The herdsman has been giving his attention to the traces— the signs of a track. Now, for the first time, the bull comes into view. It is not seen fully, nor for long. But it has been seen.

Seeing the bull means for the first time looking in a new way at our own mental activity. We begin to realize that, far more than outer happenings, it is our own moods and emotions that are influencing our sense of freedom or bondage, expansion or restriction.

These are only glimpses and we do not see the problem clearly, nor do we yet know what to do about it. All the same, this first real peep into our inner world is an essential stage in self-knowledge.

In daily life, we often tend to feel that it is other people who are restricting us. The yogic insight is: 'No. The root cause of all restriction is my own mental activity and want of understanding.' If we can accept this, we are ready to begin the training of the mind. This training, if properly carried out, will not only sharpen our awareness but will open the way to the treasury of spiritual peace at the heart of our being.

Before pondering our next picture, let us reflect briefly on what is going on. There is a bull. We have seen it. And now a choice has to be made. Do I really need to catch and tame this bull? After all, it's going to be rather demanding, and do I really need to change? Do I want to change?

Catching the Bull

A positive decision has been made. 'Yes, I must deal with this problem', which turns out to be the problem of the untrained and unenlightened mind. More specifically, the problem is how to convert the mind from its present state of restlessness and agitation to the condition of spiritual peace that I have heard about. This problem will not go away, yet time is flashing by and I have no peace, no real direction.

Something must be done.

Let us suppose that we have made the great decision: 'Yes, I will catch this bull. I will learn how to train and spiritualize my mind.' We have accepted the challenge, which is the ultimate challenge of life. Now, as you see in the picture, do not expect a smooth run. Do not expect the bull to yield to your lassoo without a struggle. There is bound to be resistance. But why is the bull furious? Simply because it is a creature of habit. It is deeply attached to the old ways, and fears the unknown. But the true welfare of the mind only comes to light when we create peace and harmony within ourselves. It is then that the mind becomes a revealer of the infinite and immortal spiritual knowledge that underlies it.

Taming the Bull

This picture shows a definite advance. The bull is on the way to becoming domesticated, that is, tamed. It is following the herdsman, who is leading it by the nose-ring. Note that the herdsman is still holding the rope and it is not a long rope. In other words, the bull is being carefully controlled, but is no longer resisting this control. It seems to be falling in with this guidance quite naturally and even contentedly.

But we must not forget the short lead. It symbolizes our need to guide the mind with alertness and care until the destination is reached. The apparent contentment of the bull suggests relief that the mind has at last found a purpose and a goal. It is now being fed with the right food and does not need to be restless or in the dark any more. The way of light and peace is open to it.

What exactly is this spiritual training and what is its purpose? The purpose of the training is to shift the mastery of the personality from the mind to the Self which underlies it. The true position is that the Self is the inner ruler of the personality, the power behind the mind. Our training restores the mind to its status as an instrument of that supreme spiritual power. The mind is meant to be a clear channel through which the divine power and peace may flow unobstructed. This crucial leverage over the mind is symbolized by the rope fixed to the bull's nose-ring. So the picture, Taming the Bull, denotes real progress, chiefly through making a spiritual use of the will.

Returning Home on the Back of the Bull

In this picture, the herdsman is calmly and joyfully riding on the back of the bull. He is no longer holding the bull, either with a rope or with reins. His hands are free and he is playing the flute. This picture symbolizes the deep change which has taken place in the mind. In yogic terms, the main expression of the mind has become *sattvic*, a Sanskrit word suggestive of peace,

100

harmony and a happiness that springs from within oneself and not from externals.

At this stage, the pupil may well feel that he has done what he set out to do. After long application and dedication, perseverance and loyalty to the path, his mind is thoroughly improved and well-controlled. But this is not the end of the journey and there are dangers lurking in this condition. The great goal of self-realization must not be forgotten or taken for granted. We must go on and penetrate the truth until we realize our identity with it. The advice is: Do not rest satisfied with the limited peace which comes to the mind. Pursue the quest until the Self is realized in its true nature as one with the Absolute. And be ready to let go of all limited ideas about yourself, even such sentiments as: 'I am established on my spiritual path. I am a servant of truth. I am dedicated to the good of others, to the good of all. I am a devotee.' These are all mental ideas centring on our individuality, but the highest truth, our spiritual destiny, transcends all conditions.

The Bull Forgotten, the Herdsman Remains

Now our herdsman-pilgrim is ready to take a further step. The main thing about this picture is that the bull is forgotten. Before now it was not forgotten. What does this mean? For a long time our efforts are concentrated on trying to create in the mind spiritual conditions. As this progress continues, inner changes take place, in the form of expansion of consciousness.

A deeper phase of our nature comes into view, revealing something of the spiritual power at the heart of our being, and its emanations of peace and light. Slowly but surely, we lose our preoccupation with our mind and its imagined virtues or imperfections. What now claims our attention and interest is the development going on at the centre of our being, which can be indicated by the term 'spiritual experience' and is of a nature that is pure, subtle and wholly superior to the stream of changing thoughts. We now know that the way forward is through attentive silence, focused on our divine centre, which is one with the Supreme. Thus we follow the path of devotion-knowledge.

The grace of a higher understanding is closer than we might imagine. It is an inner revelation of non-duality and comes as a consequence of the cultivation of the highest ideal of spiritual living. Prepared in this way, the sense of limited individuality associated with the word 'I', dissolves, and all restrictions of consciousness fall away. In an instant the truth is revealed. This realization of non-duality is the experience of the sages.

Bull and Man Both Gone Out of Sight

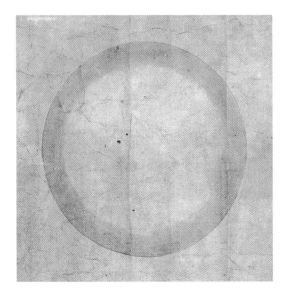

This picture suggests that the herdsman has come to the end of his journey. It is an image of empty space and indicates the transcendental nature of spiritual truth, which is beyond the range of speech and thought. There is nothing objective that can depict it, because in the end, there is nothing objective. All is Self alone and we are That.

Now there are two more pictures for us to consider. The first one is called:

The Return to the Ground and Origin

We see once more the landscape. In fact nothing seemingly has changed: the tree is still a tree, the rock is still a rock. It seems as if the world of duality has reappeared. But for the sage, and only for the sage, the vision is of quite a different quality. Before enlightenment, as it were, the world of duality, and its impression in the mind, were taken as real. Now they are known to be unreal.

When taken as real, the world of duality seems to limit the Self, to affect it, and possibly to harm it. In the experience of the enlightened sage, nothing whatsoever limits the Self, nothing affects it, there is nothing to fear—because there is nothing separate from the Self. Anything that appears does so within the Self, it has its being in the Self, and, as an appearance only, it dissolves in the Self. The sage sees with the inner eye of wisdom that this whole world of plurality is a phenomenal appearance superimposed on the canvas of infinite consciousness. The changes which take place in the names and forms create no disturbance at all in consciousness, which remains ever free and transcendent.

The final picture is entitled:

Entering the Market of the World with Open Hands

To the onlooker, the sage appears to re-enter the world of appearances, the everyday world, and mix with the people as one of them, as if engaged in a real situation. But to get a clue to the true position, we need to recall that earlier picture where bull and man had both vanished.

To the onlooker, there appear to be enlightened beings. Like the sage in the picture, they bring to mankind the spiritual food it needs in order to awaken to the realization of the same divine truth. This is a true and necessary picture from the point of view of the onlooker. The holy sages transmit to us the priceless knowledge that will enable us to transcend the limitations of life, including death, and to realize perfect, infinite freedom.

From the standpoint of the sage, there is no such situation. The realization is: Self alone is the ultimate reality, and there is no duality whatsoever. The unenlightened see the sage in different ways, according to their degree of spiritual insight. But only self-realization will reveal that one's own Self is the sole reality of the universe, and that—for purposes of self-awakening—the sage is one's own Self in apparently objective form. The sage is thus a unique means within the phenomenal world to help bring about a spiritual awakening that, in fact, exposes the unreality of the phenomenal world and establishes the absolute reality of Self as one without a second.

A man in a dream sees his body and mind harassed by a tiger. A rescuer hands him a gun and he shoots the tiger, and the relief somehow awakens him. But when he awakens, the reality of all the elements in the dream dissolves.

The sage is that particular appearance within the

realm of appearances, that can effect the liberation of those who feel they are in bondage or darkness, and are open to guidance. Such a one has the necessary understanding of the mental and physical realms that he himself has transcended. There is a definite way to transcend the apparent bondage, to dissipate the darkness. The sage is to be resorted to, and his or her teachings followed, as the way to fulfilment.

Enlightenment exposes the illusory nature of all duality, and brings to light the eternal fact of non-duality. The sage is not identified with any phase of the world appearance, nor with any role within it. To the unenlightened onlooker, the sage appears, as in the picture, to enter the market place of the world with precious spiritual gifts to offer to the people. But in himself, he is infinitude and transcendence itself, never different from the Self of the seeker.

This identity, which has its root in non-duality, is revealed once our false ideas have been dissipated. It is then that we realize directly that the completeness we have been seeking is the fully revealed nature of our innermost Self, and that we have never been anything other than That.

LIGHT FROM THE
CHANDOGYA UPANISHAD

HUMAN LIFE in this ever-changing world (*sansara*) is often compared to the struggles of a swimmer or a sailor in a vast sea, over which we have very limited power and in which we can easily drown. Yet we can be rescued from this predicament by awakening to a deeper life experience. In this deeper life experience, called enlightenment or God-realization, the world, with its complexity and menace, is robbed of its power to intimidate us. Compared to this illumined understanding, the sea of sansara is known to be an illusion, a play of surface appearances only and not a substantial reality.

The truly substantial reality is the Self of all, beyond limitations, which, in the Upanishads, is declared to be 'greater than earth... greater than heaven, greater than these worlds'. Hence, the spiritual teachers of all times and climes serve to deliver us from the turmoils of this sea of becoming, by awakening us to a deeper reality, a deeper truth, and that deeper truth is the true nature of our own Self. 'May you be successful in crossing to the farther shore beyond darkness', is the benediction of the holy Rishis, the ones who provide us with the means to this spiritual awakening.

Man, before his spiritual awakening, clings to his

own particular supports in this ocean of becoming. Each has his particular raft. Some rafts may appear huge, safe and full of attractions, like ocean-going liners. This is the raft of wealth. Other rafts seem to be slender props that we can barely hold on to; these are the rafts of poverty and destitution. Everything that we depend on for support and meaning in this sea of becoming is a kind of raft: the raft of our skills, of our knowledge; the raft of our position, the raft of our home and our relationships. But however sturdy our supports may appear to be at this moment, they do not transcend this all-surrounding ocean of transient being in which we, as transient creatures, abide and struggle during the few decades that make up the span of our life. In the words of the *Chandogya Upanishad* (VIII.12.1): 'O Indra, this body indeed is mortal. This is covered by death.' The meaning is that it is not enough for us to realize that our body is mortal; to promote true detachment, the Upanishad rouses us by saying that the body is 'covered by death' or 'grasped by death', that is, this body may die at any moment. This is one of the conditions that attend our stay in this ocean of becoming and a good reason why it is crucial to awaken to a deeper reality as soon as possible.

What can we do to banish this darkness, to escape this turbulence and uncertainty, so that our heart will be set in peace, bliss and freedom? Is there a way to transcend the sea of sansara? We can seek a solution within the sea, through manipulating conditions by skill and with the material to hand. Some may seek to build a bigger and better boat. This is the economic solution, based on wealth and possessions. Others may think more broadly and decide to rope their rafts to neigh-bouring rafts, and form a whole network of linked rafts that may more easily withstand the fitful winds and choppy waves. This is the attempt to arrive at a social and political solution. Still others may resort to praying to the God of the ocean, for peace and calm in the ocean generally, or perhaps only for the little stretch that involves their self-interest or that of their group, clan or creed. This is the religious solution. But all these solutions assume one thing: that the ocean is real, that it stands over and above us as a vast power, and that our own being is not itself the ocean, but a mere drop in it.

Do we possess a deeper faculty which, when awakened, will enable us to see beyond the sea of becoming and realize the immortal, infinite and blissful substratum of this illusion? Can we realize our essential identity with this reality and that our innermost being is never in danger of being harmed or destroyed—that there is That in us which is not 'grasped by death' and never can be? There is such a faculty, and when it is awakened, we will be identified with ultimate truth, not victims of illusion. This is the faculty of spiritual under-standing, and its end is conscious immortality.

This divine knowledge is immeasurably superior to

anything we may gain within the ocean of becoming. It is a knowledge that is not passed on lightly. In ancient times, a knower of truth imparted it only to a competent disciple who came and lived with him for the purpose of gaining the higher knowledge. 'He should not impart to anyone else at all, even though he is offered this earth surrounded by water and filled with wealth. This knowledge is greater than that; this indeed is greater than that.' (III.11.5-6)

In one of the stories found in this Upanishad, the king of the Gods, Indra, as well as the king of the demons, Virochana, come as humble petitioners for this knowledge, and Indra, who possesses everything, undergoes a long training before the subtle, imperishable truth is finally realized by him. This is the true Self-knowledge, and his guru, Prajapati, sums up its benefit when he tells Indra: 'He who, having known that Self, realizes it, attains all the worlds and all desirable things.' (VIII.12.6) That is, he is completely fulfilled and totally free from grief and want.

In the *Chandogya Upanishad*, there are several instances of one-to-one communications between teacher and pupil, and these stories indicate the attitude of mind that is necessary if we wish to learn the spiritual truth. For example, we have to approach a spiritual teacher in an attitude of humility and genuine quest. Then, the teacher will reveal the essence of the holy teachings. But if, on the part of the enquirer, there is the least

113

antagonism, suspicion or pretence, then, through an invisible spiritual law, those teachings will not pour forth; or, if they are transmitted, they will not be adequately received. The kingdom of heaven cannot be taken by storm, nor does it open its doors to those who are not prepared to approach with the guileless receptivity and absence of pride that are found in the small child. Sometimes the highest teachings are held back, giving us the chance to re-examine our motives, and prove to ourselves whether we are prepared to make the necessary adjustments to our inner and outer life, favouring the pure and liberating knowledge over personal profit and individual enhancement.

In one of the stories, it is the king, Janashruti Pautrayana, who seeks out the destitute sage, Raikva, and not vice versa. For the king has been deeply moved by the saying: 'Anyone else who knows what Raikva knows, he is also like Raikva.' Bringing great offerings, the king finds a man living under the shelter of a cart. He has to put up with Raikva's response, which is to address him: 'O Shūdra', that is, 'O, one of low caste', and with his refusal to accept the gifts. Yet the king's thirst for knowledge has dried up his personal pride. He perseveres in his quest and is given the liberating teachings. (IV. sections 1 and 2)

The sages are awake to the deeper life experience called spiritual illumination. They do not impart the knowledge of how to build a bigger raft in this ocean of becoming. Nor are their instructions primarily concerned with ways and means by which we may appeal to the God of the ocean to end our troubles and create conditions of calm in our own bit of the sea. Their sole purpose is to remove the cover from our inner spiritual eye, so that the whole experience of the present may be seen in a new light. They reveal that this ocean of becoming is in reality an ocean of pure being, one only without a second*. That essential reality, concealed behind the spectacle of constant change, hidden under the waves of names and forms, is identical with the essential being of man. In truth, we have nothing to fear, because our true nature is the All.

This awakened understanding—that our innermost being is the infinite eternal truth behind all experience, that even now we are experiencing nothing separate and unsupported by our own divine Self—has nothing to do with the extension of our physical and mental powers. These mental and physical powers are part of the transient ocean of becoming, and the seemingly individualised entity that delights in personal expansion and imagined superiority is indeed 'grasped by death'. The first lesson imparted to the pupil, Shvetaketu, by his father, a knower of truth, is that the spiritual reality is subtle; it is beyond the grasp of the intellect. This young

---

* *ekam eva advitiyam* is the Sanskrit phrase from the *Chandogya Upanishad* (VI.2.1).

man had gained much learning and had become proud
of his intellect.

> To him, the father said: 'O Shvetaketu, now that you
> are conceited, proud of being a learned man, and
> immodest like this, did you ask about that instruction
> through which the unheard becomes heard, the un-
> thought becomes thought, the unknown becomes
> known?' Shvetaketu asked: 'O venerable sir, in what
> way is that instruction imparted?' (VI.1.2-3)

In the Upanishads, the great spiritual reality underlying all appearances, the real thing, so to say, that is
appearing in the guise of millions of names and forms as
the objects of the world and the forms of our thoughts,
is called Brahman, the Absolute. The world, including
our body and mind, is not separate from the Absolute; it
is the Absolute partially or wrongly understood. It is
reality 'seen through a glass, darkly', in the phrase of St
Paul. The dark glass is the unenlightened human mind.
Anything viewed through such a glass is bound to be
darkened and distorted by the qualities of the glass. Our
higher destiny is not to be reconciled to this life of
filtered and distorted vision. It is to remove the veil, to
lift away the dark glass; that is, to transcend the picture
of reality imposed on us by the mind, and know our
oneness with the reality as it is in truth. The Upanishads
reveal that this ocean of becoming, when seen with the

eye of wisdom, is not other than the ocean of pure being, taintless existence, one without a second.

To know reality is to be reality. Enlightenment does not mean that we, as individuals, who may insist, 'I want enlightenment', will find ourselves in a position where we stand over and above the spectacle of the world and say: 'O yes, it is all pure being.' What is necessary is to learn how to dissolve the unit of our individuality itself in the pure being that is our root and source, and then the truth about all experience will be realized. This is to be awake to the knowledge of That 'through which the unheard becomes heard, the un-thought becomes thought, the unknown becomes known'.

The world is a field of appearances consisting of name, form and movement, an ocean of becoming. But what are these appearances of? They are appearances of the Absolute, the one without a second. In a sense, we already have knowledge of the Absolute. In it we live and move and have our being. But this knowledge is incomplete, like the view through the dark glass, and we have picked up the wrong impression. This wrong impression is that the world of multiplicity, this ocean of becoming, is real just as it appears to us, and that it does not stand for anything beyond itself.

The *Chandogya Upanishad* uses the example of ornaments and other objects made out of the same material. One man may collect ornaments of gold, including some finely fashioned animals. He is always conscious that all these objects—the lion in the posture of leaping, the elephant, the deer—are essentially all one, as gold. Then a child comes, who does not know about gold. All he knows is that it is such a fine lion, and he wants to play. He wants to create an adventure with the lion chasing the deer. It is all conflict and drama, and the gold, that makes all these things essentially one, is unknown as such to the child. But there is another phase of cognition, a deeper insight, which sees through the forms. If we really know gold, we know what is fundamental and true of all things made of gold; for the individual forms are perishable; they can be melted down and reformed into new shapes with different names; but the gold remains as gold throughout all these transformations.

This discernment of the essence beyond form is the means to the ultimate fulfilment of man's urge for knowledge.

O my son, as by knowing a lump of gold all things made of gold become known, all transformation has speech as its basis, and it is name only. Gold as such is the reality. (VI.1.5)

This teaching is extended to include the whole universe. What our mind and senses perceive as the perishable and ever-changing forms, are phenomenal appearances of the same underlying substance. That substance is not material at all; it is the supreme spirit, Brahman, the Absolute; and that Absolute is the underlying reality in us, our inmost Self, called Atman. Human beings are, as it were, 'objects made of gold', that is, creatures who are labelled with particular names and embodied in specific and unique forms, yet who are essentially identical with that one without a second, the divine spirit, the Absolute, Brahman, and, as the Upanishad teaches: this Atman, this Self, is Brahman.

The light of experience is Brahman alone, the Absolute, but through the medium of the human mind, experience apparently presents itself as the endless intricacies of worldly life. We have to cope with these details, and learn to live wisely in this ocean of becoming. But it is a mistake to think that there is no higher knowledge or deeper vision available to us, and that our little raft is destined to capsize while we are still in the dark.

It is true that in this ocean of becoming, we do not know what will happen next, nor can we predict what we ourselves will be thinking the next moment. All is motion, change and uncertainty. Yet the deeper reality, the gold in the objects made of gold, transcends all division and change. The Brahman-nature underlies all phenomena equally, and we can discover it by first seeking it at the core of our own being.

In one of the stories in the *Chandogya Upanishad*,

the teacher accepts a sincere pupil, but then sends him away to the forest to rear his herd of four hundred cattle and not to return until the herd has reached a thousand. The pupil, Satyakama Jabala, has such a deep yearning for true knowledge that he moves the hearts of the gods with his longing. The gods then enter non-human forms to impart to him insights about the deeper reality.

The bull tells him that each of the four directions, north, south, east and west, when truly understood, is Brahman, the Absolute, and nothing but Brahman. From the fire he learns that the earth itself, as well as the sky, the heavens and the oceans, are in reality the undivided, limitless Brahman. Similarly, he is taught by the swan that fire, the sun, moon and lightning, are, as it were, 'parts' of Brahman and have no independent existence. Finally, the diver-bird turns his attention to his own inner world. He is told that the very life-force that animates him is in reality Brahman; that the eye and the ear, through which he knows names and forms, are Brahman; that the mind itself is Brahman. For all these things are like the objects made of gold, while Brahman is the underlying reality. Satyakama is expected to meditate deeply and long on these teachings.

After years of meditation and of tending the herd, Satyakama eventually returns to the teacher's house. The teacher addresses him: 'O Satyakama, you shine verily like a knower of Brahman. Who has given you instruction?' He answers: 'Some who are other than human beings.' But he adds that it is the teacher himself who should now give him the final instructions that lead to absolute fulfilment. The story ends by saying that the teacher did indeed impart the final teachings to him, 'with nothing left out, with nothing left out'. (IV. sections 4 to 9)

One of the great teachings of the *Chandogya Upanishad* is that we need to pay close attention to our own experience, because this is where the riddle of life will be solved. This does not mean paying close attention to outer affairs, which we have to do anyway in order to stay afloat in this ocean of becoming. But at the core of every experience, there is something like a subtle essence, an invisible support, a spiritual light. It is so subtle that it is easily missed. But if we were to subtract this spiritual element from experience, the world of names and forms, of thoughts and feelings, would vanish in an instant. 'That which is the subtle essence, this whole universe has That as its Self.' (VI.8.7)

We have to discover this essence in our own being. This inner region is often called in the Upanishads 'the heart', but the term is not to be taken physically. It means the subtle realm within us where the thoughts and feelings manifest, and it may also be called 'the mind'. It is here that the true Self has to be sought for.

At first, when we seek for the Self within the realm of the mind, we are apt to think that the Self is something smaller than the mind, on the principle that anything that is said to be within something else must be smaller than its container. Conforming to our ordinary ideas about size and space, the Upanishad begins one of its verses: 'This Self of mine within the heart is smaller than a rice-seed, or a barley seed, or a seed of mustard or of millet.' This is pointing to something that is said to be even smaller than these tiny things. But then the verse continues: 'This Self of mine within the heart is greater than the earth, greater than space, greater than heaven, greater than these worlds.' (III.14.3-4)

This is a clear hint that we are not seeking anything with size at all, whether small or great. We are seeking nothing less than the supremely subtle and all-pervading spiritual principle, the essence, the invisible support of all, the spiritual light. No wonder Shvetaketu is told that he is now approaching a very different kind of know-ledge, which will enlighten him about 'that instruction through which the unheard becomes heard, the un-thought becomes thought, the unknown becomes known'.

The great and subtle principle referred to as being within the heart is Brahman, the Absolute. It is a teaching of profound significance, which has a bearing on our attitude to the whole of our experience. 'All this is Brahman' (*Sarvam Khalvidam Brahma*), as the great utterance declares. 'This universe is born from, dissolves in and exists in That. Therefore, one should meditate by becoming calm.' (III.14.1)

122

How did this ocean of pure being, one only without a second, transform itself into the ocean of becoming, and thus initiate all this multiplicity? When and where did it happen, and why? Has there really been a departure, a falling-off, from the sublime serenity of non-duality? Has perfection really become divided? Did it really happen, or is it all a special effect of the lens, the dark glass through which we apprehend experience? How real is this bondage?

When we find in the Upanishad the statement: 'In the beginning, my dear, all this universe was being alone, one only without a second,' (VI.2.1) it is not speaking of long ago. It is indicating ultimate reality here and now. This is the reality to be realized when the dark glass no longer conditions our understanding. From this standpoint of spiritual knowledge, the apparent ocean of becoming, with its waves of names and forms, is known to be an appearance only, which never affects or breaks up the essential integrity of the pure being that is the origin and basis of this appearance. The transformations have gained a pseudo-reality, through the wrong impressions and conclusions entertained by the mind that apprehends them, and the mind itself, with its continuous transformations, is in the same category. As regards this world of appearances, the Upanishad declares: 'All transformation has speech for its basis, and it is name only'. (VI.4.1) To name the golden forms as elephant, lion and deer in no way detracts from their essential nature as gold.

LIGHT FROM THE CHANDOGYA UPANISHAD

Where do we find this pure existence? In a sense it can be said to be present everywhere. It is the true substance, the thing-in-itself, which, so to say, wears the coat of the qualities that we see, hear, touch, taste and smell, but itself transcends all attributes; it is the essence that escapes all definition, the unseen ground of the seen. As Jesus said: 'I am the all, the all came forth from me and the all attained to me. Cleave a piece of wood, I am there; lift up a stone and you will find me there.' (*Gospel of Thomas,* saying 77).

The stone we have to lift is the stone of our own mind, the stone which can serve as a thick coloured lens that distorts the nature of experience, or which can be made into fine clear glass, through which the true nature of existence is revealed in all its purity and perfection. That existence is never separate from our own existence. In fact, the term existence can only be understood with reference to our own existence. We appreciate existence generally, because of our own sense of being, which can never be extinguished. We know what it is 'to be' because we know at the deepest level: 'I am'.

But what am I? Shvetaketu is told repeatedly, with the help of different illustrations (in chapter VI): 'That which is the subtle essence, all this (universe) has That as its Self. That is truth. That is the Self. That thou art, O Shvetaketu.'

The bliss and freedom of Self-realization, transmitted through the great utterance 'That thou art', are indicated in the following verse:

124

The Self indeed is below, the Self is above, the Self is behind, the Self is in front, the Self is in the South, the Self is in the North, the Self indeed is all this. Anyone who sees thus, reflects thus, understands thus, revels in the Self, sports in the Self, has union in the Self, has pleasure in the Self. He becomes a sovereign. He has freedom of movement in all the worlds. (VII.25.2)

Since the spiritual reality is one only without a second, the real meaning of this verse is that the Self is all in all. The sea of becoming is realized as the infinite ocean of pure being. There is nothing to fear, nothing to desire, because the plurality of names and forms, and the mental reactions which they stimulate, are replaced by the supreme knowledge that 'All this is Brahman' and in my true nature, I am verily That. This is the realization of non-duality that is the culmination of the teachings transmitted to us by the *Chandogya Upanishad*.

10

THE TRIUMPH OF A HERO

THE CENTRAL teaching of Adhyatma Yoga is that if we calm and purify our mind through a spiritual way of life, we will arrive at a deeper understanding of the nature of ultimate reality.

This principle is expressed in a response given by the Indian holy man, Shri Dada of Aligarh, to a questioner who took his stand on the common sense view that the world, as it impresses itself on our mind through our senses, is the only reality we know and can know. Shri Dada pointed out that our mind, in its normal worldly condition, sees only 'a small blurred part' of reality. To appreciate the whole picture, efforts must be made on spiritual lines to expand the mind, stimulate its love for infinity, and wean it from its thirst for extracting short-lived joys from finite experiences. 'Then', he told his questioner, 'your lightened mind will rise higher in the spiritual atmosphere... and I assure you, you will see more, much more.'

This 'seeing more' is not a question of seeing more in the world around us, nor is it a matter of gaining some unusual power, such as to see into the future, or to read people's minds—powers, which from the point of view of the highest wisdom, have no value at all. What is meant is the deepening of our power of spiritual vision and self-knowledge, through the awakening of our capacity to see behind the changing appearances of life, and apprehend the underlying reality.

This underlying reality transcends space and time, and words fail to do it justice. But to ease our way towards understanding its nature, we may call it 'the spiritual realm', in contrast with ordinary sensory and mental experience, which may appropriately be called 'the realm of appearances'.

This term 'the realm of appearances' is justified for at least two reasons. Firstly, we live in a world of changing forms. These include our own bodies as well as our thoughts, all of which are seen to appear, stay a while, and then disappear. Secondly, there is a more fundamental point that is established by both science and philosophy. All our information about the outer world comes to us through the channels of our sense organs. The mind selectively converts the raw sense data into a composite representation of the world. In this way, the world itself is made known to us as an image or appearance within the mind. It is an image or appearance that is ever changing. For each individual, the way the world appears is different and uniquely personal.

But the spiritual realm is not a mental image, nor does it change. It is more internal, more subtle and more abstract than thought itself. It is a realm of silence, calm and rest, a dimension without walls or boundaries, and which, when fully revealed, has been compared to an infinite ocean of pure consciousness, being and bliss.

being and bliss. Nor is the experience of this spiritual realm reserved for gifted souls. This invisible reality interpenetrates and illumines all experience, and is the conscious power underlying all minds, which are animated by a 'reflection' of that supreme consciousness, and have no independent existence.

So the purification of our mind enables us to 'see more' and to approach with increasing certainty the freedom and the peace of the spiritual realm within our own being. The climax of this process of inner clarification is the direct realization that this spiritual realm is the reality in us. It is our ultimate identity. The word 'I' is used in Yoga to indicate the nature of this reality, but, in this context, we are speaking of an 'I' that underlies our limited personality and is not itself personal or limited in any way. The training of the spiritual Yoga is to learn how to withdraw our sense of identification from the body and the mind, and to realize: 'I am infinite, immortal, ever perfect, by nature pure intelligence and bliss.'

If we acknowledge that this realm of transcendence not only exists, but is our true nature, then the reality-status of worldly experience, and of the body and mind itself, is called into question. Many philosophers, poets and religious thinkers, keenly aware of the mutability of human life, the world and the mind, challenge our right to call the physical world and its contents absolutely real. For this is the realm where all that appears—

whether plants, animals, human beings or even mighty structures like continents, planets and suns—are subject to the process of time, and will inevitably change and decay. The philosophy of Adhyatma Yoga, which is called Advaita Vedanta, shares this view. Whatever is transient, whatever has a beginning and end, cannot be called entirely real. This applies to anything which is perceived or conceived as an object of experience, including one's body, mind and the world. All are consigned to the category of the not-Self, with the strong implication that these phenomena are not wholly real. In contrast, the subtle realm of our innermost spiritual nature is not just real, but reality itself, ultimate reality, and it is one undivided principle with nothing outside or beyond it, existence-consciousness-bliss absolute by nature.

This underlying reality is the hidden support and revealer of all appearances and experiences. These passing forms and events have a semblance of reality only. Our conviction of the reality of what we are experiencing here and now has its source in our ignorance of the true nature of the Absolute.

Everything in our experience consists of a mixture of appearance and reality. Appearance depends on reality, but reality does not depend on appearance. Those who have realized the true Self know their spiritual independence of this realm of appearances. Their bodies and minds may appear to the unenlightened to act and suffer in the world and to share the same journey from the cradle to the grave. But their realization is that the true Self transcends empirical experience, and they are identified with the true Self and with nothing else.

Such a realization brings the idea of 'seeing more' to its limit, and the inspired utterances of the knowers of truth express insights that transcend the range of our normal mental experience. The enlightened have an all-embracing vision, and their statements show the philosophical detachment and cosmic overview of those who are no longer hypnotized by the realm of appearances, and have no illusions about its range or reality-status.

On the other hand, in Vedanta, it is not denied that the world appears. The realm of appearances is considered philosophically, and its relationship to the underlying reality is sometimes signified by metaphors, like the relationship of the waves to the sea or of ornaments made of gold to gold itself. But any metaphor is no more than a hint, an aid to grasping a higher truth that cannot directly be explained in words. So the world appearance is not denied by the sages of Vedanta; but they do deny that it has any independent and ultimate reality.

The way to this realization is the subject of a modern classic of Vedanta called *Triumph of a Hero*, or *Vira Vijaya* in Sanskrit, by Swami Mangalnath, a Mahatma who taught in the early part of the twentieth century. His work comprises some two hundred verses which spring from his enlightened vision of the one reality without a second, though the experience itself is beyond the realm of language. The text includes a brief survey of the world of phenomena, but always with the idea that whatever appears is part of a divine play that takes place seemingly, but not actually, within the supreme reality, one's own Self. For if one tries to pin down philosophically or logically what the world of appearances really is, it defies explanation and proves elusive. Nonetheless, everything in experience, from this enlightened standpoint, is traced back to the idea of the Self apparently sporting in the Self.

The title, *Triumph of a Hero,* suggests the idea of a spiritual struggle leading to a victory. This idea of a struggle, not as an outer crusade but as a subjective striving for self-mastery and illumination, is as ancient as man's longing to transcend bondage of any kind. The recognition of this need for an inner triumph is the turning point in man's spiritual evolution. As the English poet, Robert Browning, writes:

> When the fight begins within himself,
> A man's worth something.

The spiritual life is often conceived as a struggle to overcome old habits and widen our understanding by removing the psychological barriers that we ourselves have erected and sustained through repeated expression, and which keep us tied to material and selfish considerations.

Swami Mangalnath places the idea of spiritual struggle and achievement in a completely different context that goes right to the heart of the philosophical teaching of Yoga on appearance and reality. From the standpoint of enlightenment, man's innermost Self, which is called 'Atman' in Sanskrit, is not just real, but is reality itself. This deeper reality, when considered in its universal aspect as the power and support behind the whole universe, is called in Sanskrit 'Brahman', often translated as the Absolute, or the supreme spirit. The highest teachings of Yoga proclaim that Atman, the innermost Self of man, is in truth nothing other than Brahman, the Absolute. 'This Atman is Brahman'. *Ayam Atma Brahma.*

In the light of this realization, the infinity, immortality and reality of the spirit, or true Self, becomes a matter of direct experience, and the reality-status of the world of appearances is undermined. On the other hand, certain suggestions are given by the enlightened sages to help us live wisely in the world of appearances until we awaken to the highest truth about our real nature. One of these suggestions is that our empirical experience—our experience of the world and of ourselves as separate individuals—is the result of the workings of a divine power of illusion-making, the power called *maya.*

The image of a magical display or influence—and

one of the meanings of the word maya is magic—suggests that the origin and continued manifestation of the world is a mystery that cannot be solved by man's powers of reason. But this mystery can be dissolved through the power of spiritual vision, once we have purified our instruments of cognition and have learnt to 'see more'.

There are several verses in *Triumph of a Hero* which refer to maya and its power to superimpose a world of appearances on the underlying spiritual reality that transcends all appearance.

The supreme Self, whose nature is pure consciousness, appears in manifold forms with the help of his maya. (38)

The whole creation is merely maya and therefore inexplicable. (93)

This divine power of manifesting appearances is not to be seen as a force hostile to the spiritual light, like a kind of anti-spirit. It appears *within* the spiritual reality and the reality permeates, supports and illumines all the manifestations of maya.

Maya can in fact be viewed in two different ways. In its negative aspect, it is conceived as a power that deludes the human mind, precisely because it makes appearances seem real in themselves. When this happens, maya apparently brings about a total veiling of the spiritual truth, 'I am Brahman'. And so we find that the spiritual struggle is sometimes said to require the 'overcoming of maya', freeing oneself, as it were, from an illusion that penetrates all our experience, and makes what is unlimited, free and peaceful, seem a field of limitations, restrictions and pain.

Yet maya may also be contemplated as a power of divine origin, a source of wonder and amazement, for it unfolds this vast, beautiful and complex universe, and makes our human affairs seem so deep, interesting and authentically real. 'My maya is divine', says the Lord in the *Bhagavad Gita*. The ultimate magician who wields this magic power is the divine Lord, and yet the maya itself turns out to be no more real than the appearances it manifests.

Another similar, though not identical, concept of a force, or rather an influence, that makes our experience of reality seem finite, troubled and subject to an uncertain fate, instead of permitting us to enjoy the security and sovereignty of our deeper spiritual nature, is the concept called 'not-knowing', or 'not-knowledge'. For those familiar with the Sanskrit terms, we refer to *ajnana*, or its synonym, *avidya*. The words *jnana* and *vidya* both mean knowledge; the prefix 'a' changes the meaning to 'not-knowing'. In *Triumph of a Hero*, Swami Mangalnath gives pride of place to the term 'ajnana', although 'avidya' also appears in some verses. They have the same meaning and significance.

Just like maya, this 'not-knowing' appears to be an event that occurs within the divine consciousness itself. The infinite consciousness, which is all-in-all and is nothing but perfection, knowledge and light, appears to undergo a condition of limitation. This apparent finitisation of the Infinite is due to ajnana, or not-knowing, which has its locus, so to say, in the infinite consciousness itself.

This concept of ajnana, not-knowing, that appears to overpower the perfect infinite spirit of man, is introduced in the sixth verse of *Triumph of a Hero*, and, as we shall see, it has a lot to answer for! This is because ajnana is conceived as the fundamental error at the heart of our experience, and the one which conditions human life in its unenlightened phase.

> Atman (the innermost Self) having been overpowered by his own ajnana and conceiving Himself to be of a different nature, in Himself and for Himself bursts forth in forms different from Himself. (6)

If the ultimate and natural experience is one of spiritual perfection, unmarred by the vicissitudes of the world of appearances, then it would appear that something has happened to interfere with, and even to spoil, this unbroken perfection. The teaching of Yoga is that the perfection at the core of experience is not really marred or tainted, but remains in transcendent glory. But from our standpoint as spiritual enquirers, something seems to have happened that has brought us to our present discontented state. In the spiritual philosophy, this apparent fall from grace is attributed to spiritual ignorance, or ajnana.

How real is this so-called happening, this rise of an influence within the perfect infinite spirit that causes the appearance of forms other than itself? The ultimate standpoint is that this happening is not real at all. The clue to this is contained in the very word which seems to cause all the trouble: ajnana—not-knowing. For if there is a not-knowing that is responsible for veiling the true nature of reality, and putting in its place this bitter-sweet world of ups and downs, life and death, might there not be a *knowing* that reverses the vision? The practical purpose of Adhyatma Yoga is to bring about this higher knowledge.

Pure knowledge, perfect, complete and un-obstructed, is the very nature of our innermost Self. The aim of spiritual enquiry and practice is to negate the coverings and confusions that have been worked up through ajnana, or 'not-knowing'. This is traditionally achieved through calming and purifying the mind, and listening to teachings that ignite our recognition of our real nature and seek to awaken us to what we really are. If we follow this method, there will come a time when our spiritual Self, which is the only truly conscious element in our experience, 'hears in a right way the statements about its true nature' (verse 37). It is then that Atman realizes its freedom from the influence of ajnana or not-knowing, and abides in its own glory.

In the spiritual expression of mankind, the idea of a struggle usually denotes the endeavours of an individual seeker who, in the end, is rewarded with the prize of enlightenment or salvation, depending on which spiritual tradition is being explored. But this particular model does not fit the more metaphysical exposition found in *Triumph of a Hero.* For here the so-called hero is none other than the supreme reality itself, Atman, the deeper, spiritual Self in all human beings and their divine ground. The triumph is the negation of that strange influence called ajnana, or not-knowing, which apparently forms itself within the reality and gives rise to the world of appearances.

In the light of this victory, that is, the negation of not-knowing, all the manifested effects of not-knowing, including the rise of the sense of individuality and the unfolding of the world of relativity, are understood to be unreal appearances, which never at any stage impose a real limitation on the reality of Atman.

Swami Mangalnath uses various superlatives to indicate this supreme spiritual victory of the Self realizing itself, as it were. He calls it an absolute victory, the greatest triumph, the endless glory, the never-ending bliss, the abiding in one's eternally established sovereignty. This realization is so comprehensive that it sweeps away all sense of having participated in any war or struggle at all. Thus the divine experience is not marred even by a retrospective sense that a struggle has taken place. Instead there is the conviction expressed in verses 132-134:

> What bliss that I have now come to remember that whatever existed in the past was verily my own Self, and whatever I knew was indeed my Self-cognition!

> Whatever I saw was verily my own form; whatever I heard, that, too, was my own Self!

> I was, I am and I shall be! Nothing other than Myself ever was or is now or ever shall be! Such is the conviction of the natural hero, abiding forever in his own glory.

So far this account of the spiritual life has been presented as a drama which takes place within the supreme reality, Atman, our true Self, and nowhere else, and which turns out to be a pseudo-drama, a kind of fiction or imagination and not a true historical event. On the other hand, from the point of view of the limited individual, the struggle for self-transcendence seems real enough, and so does the worldly environment which forms its background setting. *Triumph of a Hero* does include verses that appreciate the individualised stand-point, yet which help us to reflect on our own experience and situation in the light of the highest teachings.

We might, for example, ask how it is that human individuality arose in the first place, if it is ultimately meant to be transcended? Or, to put it another way, why is it that experience, that is meant to be free and infinite, always seems to be filtered and restricted by an individualised ego associated with a particular body and mind? Echoing the explanation given by the classical teacher Gaudapada, Swami Mangalnath sees the rise of the sense of individuality as the very first effect of this not-knowing which appears to have 'happened' in the true Self.

> First Atman (the real Self) imagines Himself as a jiva (a separate individual soul), whose nature is to act and to experience. Then, by way of emphasizing the condition of individuality, He imagines entities of various kinds, who also appear to be active and conscious beings. Then, he remembers his experiences of these imagined entities, and these memories lead to fresh experiences. (Verse 30)

The verse draws our attention to what was referred to earlier as the fundamental error at the heart of our experience, an error which results in our conviction that we are separate individuals.

By calling the sense of individuality an error, we may seem to be denying an obvious fact of experience. But there are reasonable explanations as to how the sense of individuality is itself a secondary element in experience, and how it serves as an illusory and illogical covering of our true nature as the infinite spiritual Self. For example, the infinite spiritual Self is sometimes indicated by the affirmation 'I', 'I', 'I', unlinked to any particular conditions or qualities. We can then imagine the descent into individuality when the affirmation of the simple 'I' is joined with the word 'am' to become 'I am'. The 'I am', unless we deliberately identify it with the pure 'I', will arouse limited associations. No sooner do we feel 'I am', than we attach to it the qualities of our body, mind, mood, circumstances, and so on.

Among the characteristics we attach to the 'I' is the sense of our involvement in action and worldly experience. We convince ourselves that it is our very nature 'to act and to experience', in company with innumerable other people, who, we feel, are in the same position. In this way the play of subject-object experience gains intensity and complexity. During this process, we forget the pristine and infinite nature of the true I.

This false identification is the basic error or confusion at the heart of experience, and it is based on ajnana, or not-knowing the deeper truth about our own being.

Swami Mangalnath briefly refers to one or two of the most significant convictions of human beings while they are under this limiting influence. For example there is the characteristic desire for limited experiences and objects:

This Atman, who is the ocean of eternal bliss, becoming thirsty for the drops of worldly pleasures on account of indifference to recognition of his own nature, fluctuates like a water-wheel rising and falling in a well. (50)

And again, there is the sense of guilt or sin:

Afflicted with suffering, He cries, 'I am a sinner! Because I have committed sin, my nature has become soiled with sin! O God, protect me!' (49)

These, and similar restrictive ideas and feelings about ourselves, bear no relation to what we are in our true nature, which is self-illumined, without a veil, perfect bliss, infinite and independence itself. A good part of our spiritual practice and enquiry is to learn to sift away false ideas about our essential nature, and affirm that our true Self is the spiritual reality and not conditioned by any qualities or limitations at all.

So much for the roots of our individuality. What about the world in general? The world itself is also an appearance within the deeper reality of the true Self, Atman, projected by the influence of ajnana or not-knowing, an influence which owes its existence to the ultimate reality and to nothing else. It is this spiritual reality, when spoken of in the cosmic sense as the support of the world appearance, that is called

'Brahman', denoting magnitude or greatness. To the enlightened, all that apparently comes within experience is intrinsically Brahman, from whom it derives its power to manifest and appear real.

Therefore we find that certain terms are used synonymously. Atman (the Self), Brahman (the Absolute) and also words indicating God, such as the Lord, are not essentially different concepts, but express one and the same underlying reality. Here, for example, is a verse which equates Atman with the Lord, as the ultimate principle which manifests the universe, 'protects' it while it endures, and into which it is finally withdrawn:

> This whole universe is Atman alone. It is the Lord alone who creates and is created, who protects and is protected, who withdraws and is withdrawn. (106)

When we realize that the world is an illusory appearance superimposed on a deeper reality, we can say with conviction: 'All is verily Brahman', or 'All is Atman alone'. For the one who realizes the supreme truth, everything within the range of experience is real in the sense that its underlying reality is plainly evident. For the goldsmith, all the objects made of gold are essentially nothing but gold. But if, through not knowing the truth about the underlying reality, we take our experience at face value, our mental and sensory experiences may justifiably be called unreal, because they comprise a sequence of transient appearances, and we have not yet identified ourselves with the permanent divine ground on which these passing manifestations come and go. This sublime wisdom is expressed in the following verses:

> All is real as Brahman (the supreme spiritual reality) and as different from Brahman is unreal. Thus alone can the holy truth be described, and not otherwise. (190)

> That which is superimposed (the world of appearances) derives its existence from the substratum (the spiritual ground on which it appears). It is non-existent if considered apart from the substratum. (194)

The ideas on reality and appearance that are expressed in *Triumph of a Hero* are not presented as dogmas that shun personal enquiry and questioning. They are the outcome of a profound analysis of human experience, aided by the insights gained when the human mind is rendered serene, pure and clear. There is a way of reflecting on one's own experience in order to distinguish between what is passing and perishable, and what is permanent and transcends the process of change. The conclusion, derived from spiritual insight, is that our innermost consciousness is unchanging and transcendent, and all else is appearance.

The highest expression of spiritual truth identifies

this innermost consciousness of man with the supreme reality, Brahman, the Absolute, and is transmitted through the 'great sentences' of the Upanishads, such as 'I am Brahman'—*Aham Brahmasmi.* This is inspired revelation, transcending reason. Yet the Vedanta philosophy, through reason, establishes that any other view of man's nature is incomplete and does not open a way to the highest good. The advice to the spiritual enquirer is:

> Silence is best, but if you have to say something of it, then speak carefully and reasonably, otherwise people will not respect a thesis unwarranted by reason. (188)

There is something much higher than reason that comes into operation when we gain true spiritual understanding, that is, when 'Atman hears in a right way the statements about Atman, and, freeing Himself from the influence of avidya and its effect, the world, induces in Himself the state of transcendence.' (37) This hearing in the right way is a deeper power within us, which only comes into operation when the mind, intellect and feelings have been effectively silenced. The faculty that reveals to us the highest truth, and effects our ultimate triumph over ignorance, over not-knowing, is the higher faculty of spiritual intuition.

Once we have decided that the spiritual teachings are reasonable and relevant to our own quest for higher knowledge, it becomes possible to hear them in a spirit of receptivity, of openness, without irrelevant ideas and reactions causing interference. A reference to the transmission of living truth comes in verse 201:

> Sometimes these expressions spontaneously issue forth from an illumined man, and the ignorant, on hearing them, give up ascribing selfhood to the not-Self.

In this way, the fundamental error at the heart of human experience is brought to an end. The cloud of not-knowing, that appears to veil the innermost truth, is dissipated, and Atman realizes its true nature:

> Atman is verily His own friend when he assumes His real nature: then He sees Himself free from both bondage and freedom. (112)

The natural peace of the supreme reality is re-established, along with the conviction that there never was an enemy to spoil that peace, nor a struggle to recover it.

11

THE PRACTICE OF MEDITATION (2)

MEDITATION is the most effective means for turning the mind inwards in order to discover the immutable consciousness at its source. This discovery confers on us peace, lasting happiness, freedom and an illumined understanding about the purpose of life and the nature of ultimate truth.

Meditation also brings relief from the ordinary stresses and troubles of life, by lifting our mind out of them for a time. But the real aim of meditation—its supreme value—is to prepare the mind to realize the infinite consciousness which is the ground of our being, and thus find a tranquil joy that needs nothing outer to create or sustain it, because it is the nature of our own true Self.

That higher nature is existence-consciousness-bliss absolute (*sat-chit-ananda*). It is undiscovered because we may not have been told about it or how to seek for it; or, even if we are familiar with this wisdom, we may not have understood how to apply the teachings to ourselves. Besides, our attention is often monopolised by the outer concerns, allowing us little or no time or inclination to reflect on whether there might be something deeper in life than this realm of action, enjoying and suffering.

But when we do start to raise such questions, we are

on the threshold of the path of inner unfoldment. We become spiritual enquirers—seekers after divine truth. And this direction, this new path, if we persevere, leads us into the light of conscious immortality.

To turn our thoughts and feelings to this deeper level of our being, we need a peaceful mind and one that is alert and receptive. To prepare ourselves, we approach our meditation in an attitude of reverence and calmness. Reverence makes us open-minded—open to higher values and guidance. The spiritual principle is the underlying reality, our own deeper Self, so we bow before it in reverence and humility. Let us do this for a minute or so.

Now the breathing practice. Adopting the meditation posture, using either a chair or a cushion, sit upright so that the current of breath flows without tension or tightness. We open ourselves to the light and bliss of higher knowledge, replacing any trace of tension with spiritual power and peace. Our breathing practice will incorporate the mental repetition of the holy syllable OM. (For the meaning of OM, see Chapter Seven.)

Breathe slowly and deeply, mentally repeating the holy syllable OM, hearing the sound O on the in-breath and M on the out-breath.

The OM is not voiced but 'heard' interiorly through associating the natural sound of the in-breath with 'O', and the exhalation with 'M'. In this way, we let thoughts be replaced with the pure light, peace and security transmitted through the word OM. Spend four to five minutes on this breathing practice.

The life of spiritual unfoldment begins when we learn consciously to examine, and accept or reject wisely, the thoughts and suggestions that arise in our mind. We can learn to live in good thoughts and good feelings, and, with a little training, turn aside any thoughts that threaten to depress us or make us agitated. So our next practice is:

> Give free scope to your mind to think, but whatever idea the mind brings before you, say: 'It is an illusion. I do not want it.'

This exercise will prove invaluable to those seeking to develop peace of mind and the power of spiritual concentration. Let us consider some of its implications.

Thoughts and desires arise, sometimes unexpectedly, based on the impressions we have been exposed to during the day, or from deeper psychological causes. But we need not be drawn into these thoughts if they are not helpful to us. They have no real power over us. It is our choice how we respond. We have the power, from our will, and also from the power that springs from the highest in us—our spiritual nature, the inner ruler of the personality.

We observe the thoughts as their supervisor. We accept them or quietly dismiss them if irrelevant to the task in hand or unhelpful to our spiritual progress. We address our thoughts with this authority—and we will find that with dedicated practice, any thought can be cleared from the mind, or, if we like, postponed. It is to help us establish this vital inner skill that we do this practice. And so:

When the first thought comes before you, say: 'It is illusory.' When the next thought comes, 'It is illusory' and so on...

Let us also note that, philosophically, the thoughts in themselves manifest as transient appearances, and in this sense, do behave like passing illusions. But what is real is the witnessing consciousness, and this is constant and eternal—the clue to our divine nature.

With calmness and authority, enter into this practice. Allow the thoughts to arise. Be wakeful and alert. From your inner vantage point as the witness, see what is happening on the stage of the mind, and when a thought appears, whatever its content, say: 'It is an illusion. I do not want it.' In this way, we gain mastery over the mental activity, the ability to initiate thought or redirect it as we choose—a skill we will find invaluable for meditation and for life.

The ability to dismiss thoughts is crucial for spiritual

illumination. This is because the mind, with its unending activity, forms a kind of veil that prevents the light of truth from shining through. The 'not wanted' practice thins this veil.

Our will is obviously engaged in this practice, but it is not intended to be a mechanical, robot-like rejection of thoughts. It is more a matter of conscious, intelligent observing and dismissing. Let us do this now for five minutes.

> Give free scope to your mind to think, but whatever idea the mind brings before you, say: 'It is an illusion. I do not want it.'

The mind, when congested with work-a-day thoughts, is rather like a pond covered in weeds which block the reflection of the sun. Clear the weeds and the pond once again takes the reflection of sun and sky—of light and infinity. This hints at what happens in the mind when the veil of thoughts is thinned and removed. The deeper truth is reflected in our intellect.

What is this deeper truth? This is indicated in the meditation text.

OM

TAKE UP THE MIRROR OF THY STILLED HEART
AND LOOK AT THE REFLECTION OF INFINITY IN IT.
THIS IS WISDOM, THIS IS BLISS.

OM

Empirical knowledge is gained through endowing our intellect with facts, ideas and techniques. The knowledge of imperishable truth is the essence of our being. It is not acquired; it is ever achieved. Enshrined in the depth of our being, this higher wisdom comes to light in inner stillness. Our mind, when stilled, becomes a reflector of the infinitude within.

Note that the meditation text assumes our mind is already stilled—'Take up the mirror of thy stilled heart' —and that infinity is mirrored in it now. This is the true spirit of meditation: to feel, 'It is so—yes, it is so, right now.'

So again, we apply our authority. We take up the meditation text and repeat it inwardly a few times. Then either contemplate the meaning of the text as a whole, or choose a particular word or phrase as the focus of attention. When the mind drifts into irrelevant thoughts, gently yet firmly bring it back to the meditation text, which is based on truth and the experience of those who have matured the practice of meditation. Allow ten minutes for this practice.

Our efforts to pacify and uplift our mind do have effects which go beyond our personal consciousness, just as a little light, though apparently localised, spreads all around.

This principle is well stated by Confucius:

When there is peace in the heart,
there is peace in the home.
When there is peace in the home,
there is peace in the neighbourhood.
When there is peace in the neighbourhood,
there is peace in the city.
When there is peace in the city,
there is peace in the nation.
When there is peace in the nation,
there is peace in the world.

Such is the effect of peace in the heart.

To close our meditation period, let us spend a few
moments sharing our peace of heart by offering thoughts
of unconditional goodwill to all.

12

TRUE CHRISTIANITY AND YOGA

THERE IS basic oneness of the teachings of Christ with those of Adhyatma Yoga. Consider the opening words of the *Gospel of St John*:

> In the beginning was the Word, and the Word was with God, and the Word was God. The same was in the beginning with God. All things were made by him; and without him was not any thing made that was made. In him was life; and the life was the light of men. And the light shineth in darkness; and the darkness comprehended it not.

These verses indicate that the whole cosmos is divine in origin, and that divinity is the source of light and life. The same message is found in the Upanishads. There, the great reality is called Brahman, meaning the Absolute or the supreme spirit.

> All this is Brahman. This universe is born from, dissolves in and exists in That. Therefore, one should meditate by becoming calm.
>
> *Chandogya Upanishad*, III.14.1

This truth underlies our experience in the universe. It transcends the mind, but there is a spiritual faculty in us, a latent power hidden within the mind, which, when awakened, will enable us to realize ultimate truth directly and be free forever.

Words are formulated by the mind. Both the mind and its store of words belong to the transient universe. The scriptures point to the immutable spiritual principle underlying the realm of change. This is the transcendent Absolute, and it is the whole. It is our real being. The way to its realization is through deepening self–knowledge.

The infinite and transcendent nature of this ultimate light of spiritual reality is indicated in this verse from the *Mundaka Upanishad* (II.ii.10):

> There the sun does not shine, nor the moon, nor the stars, nor do these flashes of lightning, what to speak of fire. Through His shining, everything else shines. By His light everything is lit.

In the Upanishads, words are used to lift our mind to a realm that is beyond words. In the Christian tradition, great art also attempts to raise our mind to a realm that is beyond form. Consider the nativity painting by Geertgen tot Sint Jans. There are the forms, yet there is a mysterious light that transcends the forms, symbolized by the self-luminous form of the child Christ. Is not the artist attempting to indicate the supreme source of light through which all else is lit?

In the *First Epistle of John* (1:5), this light is declared to be the very nature of God: 'God is light, and in him there is no darkness at all.' This light is man's origin and true nature.

Nativity (detail), c.1490, Geertgen Tot Sint Jans
© National Gallery, London

In the *Gospel of Thomas* (50), Jesus says:

> If they say to you: 'From where have you originated?',
> say to them: 'We have come from the Light, where the
> Light has originated through itself.'

The light which lights our mind, and the light of God,
are the same when rightly understood. Of this supreme
light, it is said in the *Chandogya Upanishad* (III.13.7):

> Now, that light which shines beyond this heaven,
> beyond the whole creation, beyond everything in the
> highest worlds which are unsurpassingly good, it is
> certainly this which is the light within a person.

We can realize this light because, in the words of John,
it is 'the true light which lighteth every man that cometh
into the world'. (1:9) The nature of this realization is
signified by Jesus, when, as recorded by Thomas (24),
he says:

> Within a man of light there is light and he lights the
> whole world. When he does not shine, there is
> darkness.

There is a supreme spiritual knowledge, an awakened
and illumined understanding, which is not different from
this ultimate light. Though transcendent, this light is

intimately present in all our experiences. All our mental conceptions and perceptions, our thoughts and feelings, are revealed by this ultimate light. If this light were absent, there would be no experience. But this light is never absent and there is nothing outside it to be absent from.

Our life experience appears to contradict this vision of truth, and this is why the holy scriptures are valued: they throw light on the spiritual reality. They are sources of higher knowledge of the Imperishable. So too are the teachings of the illumined sages who have realized the truth. The final authority is one's own experience, once the apparent obstacles to enlightenment have been removed. This divine knowledge does not reveal itself in us while our mind remains intensely active and consumed in the outer affairs. Hence the *Chandogya Upanishad* advises us: 'Therefore, one should meditate by becoming calm.'

To become calm, the mind needs to enter the inner silence with a sense that it is entering the divine presence—the source of all peace and tranquillity.

The supreme truth is to be discovered as the essence of our own being. It is approached through the contemplation of some image or symbol that indicates, in a finite and imaginable form, the infinite spiritual reality that lies within and beyond the symbol. Our focus may be in the form of a sentence or word, a sacred picture or a holy name. All such inner focusing has the aim of awakening our faculty of spiritual intuition. This is the spirit of the *Bhagavad Gita* verse, where the Lord, in the form of Shri Krishna, gives us, in words, a symbolic indication of his nature and, by implication, our own true nature, as the source of all:

> I am the source of all. From Me everything evolves. Thus thinking, the wise worship Me, endowed with contemplation. (10:8)

When Jesus declares: 'The kingdom of heaven is within you', he is providing us with a symbolic meditation designed to turn our gaze from the outer and engage us on the inner quest for self-realization.

If we want self-realization, this inner quest should be the main intention of our life. For if we seek it above everything else, we shall find fulfilment. 'But seek ye first the kingdom of God, and his righteousness; and all these things shall be added unto you.' (*Matthew*, 6:33)

The *Chandogya Upanishad* compares this spiritual realm within us to a golden treasure buried in the ground, which we may walk over again and again without realizing its nearness and availability. In the Gospels, the kingdom of heaven is also compared to a treasure that is buried in a field. The seeker is like one who has realized that this is the place where the treasure is to be sought and found. He sells everything he has and buys the whole field.

One can interpret the whole field as the mind, in which is hidden the treasure of the supreme truth as its very source. 'Buying the field' and making sacrifices to do so, signifies our determination to cultivate our mind, through tranquillity and purity, charging it with thoughts that point to our divinity. Thus the mind prepares itself for the revelation of the true nature of the light which is its source. This process is brought about by such practices as meditation, worship, service and philosophical reflection on the spiritual truth.

What is the result of this seeking? Concerning this quest, Jesus says:

> Let him who seeks, not cease from seeking until he finds, and when he finds, he will be troubled, and when he has been troubled, he will marvel, and he will reign over the All. (*Gospel of Thomas*, 2)

Once we have been told that the Lord is our true Self and is to be sought within our own heart, and we accept it; once we find, so to say, that this is where truth has to be realized, we will be troubled, because we will be faced with an inner challenge which we cannot evade. We may postpone the quest or delay it, but it will always haunt our conscience. For we can no longer claim to be ignorant of the path we have to follow. There are no longer any excuses to hold us back, or, if we have been deflected from the path, to stop us from making a new beginning. Sooner or later we will have to face our inner state and take responsibility for removing the rust from the mirror of our heart and clear our vision of egoism and self-deception.

But once our vision is cleared, even partially, we will marvel at the inner revelation. We will realize that the source of happiness and divinity is our own essential being. Finally, we will know that there is no divinity other than our true Self, our Atman, the pearl of great price. And we will recognise our Self as ever free, fulfilled and beyond all fear. Sings the sage in the *Avadhut Gita*:

> That God, Atman, by whose power the whole universe is born, in which it abides and to which it finally returns, like bubbles and waves in the sea, is realized by the wise.

Such verses remind us of the overall purpose of both Christianity and the spiritual Yoga. It is to awaken us to direct experience of reality, whether we call it 'the realization of the kingdom of heaven within', or we refer to it as *Brahmavidya*—the knowledge of Brahman, or Self-realization.

Religions are means to an end that ultimately transcends religion. They provide the dynamic and progressive steps to Self-realization. As Jesus says: 'If you bring forth that within yourselves, that which you have will save you.' (*Thomas,* 70). To bring forth what is within ourselves is to discover that our deeper Self is the source of joy. When we finally understand that we are not going to find lasting happiness in the outer world, one option still remains. And that undertaking is grounded on truth, not illusion. It is to seek the treasure within oneself, to dig in our own field. At last our joy will be full, independent, pure and peaceful. This natural joy is also the promise of Adhyatma Yoga:

> With the self (i.e. the mind) unattached to external contacts, he finds the joy which is in the Self. With the self engaged in the contemplation of Brahman, he attains the endless joy. (*Bhagavad Gita*, 5:21)

People sometimes say that they belong to a religion. This idea of belonging should not blind us to the fact that the goal of religion is transcendence and universality—freedom from all limitations. This is implicit in Jesus's teaching that the Sabbath is made for man, not man for the Sabbath. Religion, if rightly practised, purifies the mind. In that inner purity, the higher insight or wisdom arises, and that wisdom is its own authority.

In the Indian tradition all scriptural texts, including the Vedas, are acknowledged to be means to an end that transcends words, scriptures and spiritual symbols. When the truth is realized, the scriptures have served their purpose. In the words of Krishna:

An enlightened knower of truth does not need the Vedas. In the midst of an all-encompassing flood of water, one does not need a reservoir.

(*Bhagavad Gita*, 2:46)

We also need to recognise that in the spiritual life there is the state of preparation and the state of achievement. During our period of preparation, we draw the greatest comfort and aid from following what is laid down in the holy scriptures. If we want to grow spiritually, there is guidance in the scriptures and from those with spiritual light, on how to live and how to worship, how to give, to pray and to meditate, and, not least, how to overcome egoism and pretence.

The Gospels and the *Bhagavad Gita* remind us that it is the spirit of sincerity which is to be cultivated and which will help us on the path. In order to outwit the limited ego, Jesus advises us to do our spiritual practices, not for reputation or the admiration of others, but to effect a deeper communion with the indwelling Lord. (*Matthew*, 6:1-18)

When you do some act of charity, do not announce it with a flourish of trumpets, as the hypocrites do.

Instead, 'Do not let your left hand know what your right hand is doing.' In other words, do your charity without pride and afterwards forget about it.

So too when you fast, do not look gloomy. Instead, anoint your head and wash your face, so that men may not see that you are fasting, but only your Father who is in the secret place.

The same spirit of sincere striving for God or truth pervades the *Bhagavad Gita*:

When one offers to Me with devotion a leaf, a flower, a fruit, water—that I accept, offered with devotion by the pure-minded.

Whatever you do, whatever you eat, whatever you sacrifice, whatever you give, in whatever austerity you engage, do it as an offering to Me.

Thus you will be liberated from the bonds of action, which are productive of good and evil results. Equipped in mind with the yoga of renunciation and liberated, you will come to me. (9:26-28)

This reality of God or the true Self seems to be unknown, but it is not so. St Paul told the people of Athens, who had set up an altar to the unknown God, that this apparent unknownness is a delusion and that the Godhead is close at hand, for 'in Him we live, move and have our being'. (*Acts,* 17:22-29) In the *Gospel of Thomas*, Jesus is asked by his disciples: 'When will the new world come?' He replies: 'What you expect has come, but you know it not.' (51) And again, 'The

163

Kingdom of the Father is spread upon the earth and men do not see it.' (113) When Jesus says in the same Gospel, 'I will give you what eye has not seen and what ear has not heard,' (17) his words echo those of the *Chandogya Upanishad*, where the sage speaks of his instruction as shedding light on That 'through which the unheard becomes heard, the unthought becomes thought, the unknown becomes known.'

If the spiritual truth is our origin and true nature, and we live, move and have our being in this infinite ocean of light, why does this supreme truth escape our understanding, so that we have eyes, yet do not see its glory and immediacy? One explanation is that this innate wisdom of the spirit, immediate and direct as our own Self, is hidden, as it were, by our desires for other things.

> As fire is surrounded by smoke, as a mirror by rust, as the foetus is enclosed in the womb, so is spiritual wisdom covered by desire. (*Bhagavad Gita*, 3:38)

This inner blindness is cured when we develop the master desire for spiritual liberation. When the desire for liberation is dominant and we nourish it, we gain a realistic understanding of the range and limits of what we can expect from the world. We see through its glamour and are no longer deluded by its false promises. The same teaching is indicated by Jesus when he says:

Lay not up for yourselves treasures upon earth, where moth and rust doth corrupt, and where thieves break through and steal. But lay up for yourselves treasures in heaven... For where your treasure is, there will your heart be also. (*Matthew,* 6:19-21)

We need to collect the treasures of the spiritual life, that is, to cherish the sayings of the wise and to follow those practices that make our inner being peaceful and harmonious. Then, like a flame, the energy of our desires will become unified, focused and full of light.

There is another explanation why this supreme spiritual reality appears to be unknown to us. In the *Bhagavad Gita,* Shri Krishna reveals that human nature is subject to a kind of illusion called *maya* or *yoga maya*. It is this cosmic illusion, which has its source in the human mind, that veils from us the knowledge of ultimate truth. In the words of Krishna:

I am not manifest to all, veiled (as I am) by *yoga maya*. This deluded world knows not Me, unborn and imperishable... All beings are subject to illusion at birth. (*Bhagavad Gita*, 7:25 and 27)

The effect of this *maya* or illusion is that we become hypnotized by the magic show of life and have no care

165

to look deeper than the surface or to thirst for any deeper truth.

In the *Gospel of Thomas* (28), Jesus speaks of this blindness of heart as a kind of drunkenness, which impels us to cling to worldly things as if they were the only reality, even though our stay in this world is short and uncertain, and nothing material can be taken with us when we depart from here. To know ourselves truly is to be free from illusion, and to live in everlasting freedom, absolute security and fearlessness. 'Whoever knows the all, but fails to know himself, lacks everything.' (67) Where is the divinity in us? It is our Self. This is the liberating insight revealed to us by the knowers of truth. To know oneself truly is to know that behind the limited 'I', which is the individualised ego, is the transcendental Self, one without a second.

Jesus's own use of the word 'I' points to a selfhood that transcends the physical body and also the entire empirical realm of time, space and causation. 'Before Abraham was, I am.' (*John*, 8:58) And in the *Gospel of Thomas* (77), we read:

I am the Light that is above them all, I am the All, the All came forth from Me and the All attained to Me. Cleave a (piece of) wood, I am there; lift up a stone and you will find Me there.

Our innermost Self transcends all change. Being pure

166

spirit, it is enclosed by nothing. This is the Self to be enquired into for the purpose of realization, the pearl of great price, the treasure concealed in the field of the mind. When Jesus speaks in the *Gospel of St John* (chapter 17) of his own Self abiding within his disciples, and the Self of his disciples being one with his own Self, it is the same limitless selfhood that is taught by Krishna, and which applies to all beings without exception.

> The Self abiding in all beings, and all beings abiding in the Self, sees he whose Self has been made steadfast by Yoga, who everywhere sees the same.

> He who sees Me everywhere and sees everything in Me, to him I vanish not, nor to Me does he vanish. (*Bhagavad Gita*, 6:29-30)

The purpose of the spiritual Yoga is to help us to withdraw our attention from the transient contents that appear in our consciousness, and to focus our mind on that spiritual element which is the source of our being. This apparent narrowing of our focused attention on, so to say, a single point within us, leads to an expansion of consciousness beyond all imagination. As we go deeper within, we become increasingly aware of that centre of original being and radiant power. Jesus speaks of this single-minded concentration on the spiritual element within us, when he says: 'If thine eye be single, thy whole body shall be full of light'. (*Matthew*, 6:22) The meaning is, when our mind is freed from the multiplicity of worldly thoughts, our inner being will be flooded with the light that emanates from our true Self.

Another work of art from the Christian tradition which suggests this illumined inwardness of consciousness is Pieter Brueghel's *Death of the Virgin.*

Death of the Virgin (detail) c.1564, Pieter Brueghel the Elder
Upton House © NTPL

This painting shows the moment when Mary, the mother of Christ, leaves her body. One of the disciples holds a candle. But the physical light of this candle is drowned in the spiritual radiance that emanates from Mary. Illumined by the light within her, this image is not one of sorrow and loss, but depicts one who has discovered the utmost joy and freedom. The ordinariness and intimacy of the environment remind us that this light is available to all, and can be awakened through turning our attention within in one-pointed absorption in our spiritual source. This turning within for peace and light is the essence of Adhyatma Yoga. In the words of Krishna:

> When the well-restrained thought is established in the Self only, without longing for any of the objects of desire, then one is said to be *yukta* (absorbed). (*Bhagavad Gita*, 6:18)

What do our efforts lead to? The time comes when we realize that the Self is the ultimate source of attraction. Its influence becomes perceptible to a higher part of our mind. When this happens, we naturally desire to turn within for bliss, peace and light. The practice of focusing our mind on that which is spiritual within us, brings about the true conversion.

The real meaning of the word 'conversion' is given by St Paul when he wrote: 'And be not conformed to this world: but be ye transformed by the renewing of your mind.' (*Romans*, 12:2) It calls for a change of heart, a new spiritual understanding, and not a change from one religion to another. Real conversion always centres on our inner life. It involves what we are willing to do and what we actually do in order to adjust the expression of our thoughts and feelings, so that we are able to receive more and more light from our spiritual centre, our deeper Self. This process is ongoing until final illumination.

We can make progress through right thought at any given moment. The spiritual teachings are full of awakening insights, and feed the mind with ideas that uplift, purify and help to open the inner eye of wisdom. Jesus calls this inner nourishment the bread of life.

In the *Gospel of St John* (chapter 10), Jesus refers to himself as the good shepherd. We, too, have to become a good shepherd, not as a leader of others, but as a good shepherd tending the flock of our own thoughts. We have to make sure our mental herd grazes in the best pastures, and to rescue and draw back any sheep (i.e. thoughts) that leave the safe and nourishing field. The Lord within is the ultimate ruler of the personality. He is the shepherd of the flock (i.e. the mind). And the intellect is like a trained sheepdog that skilfully rounds up the sheep. The equivalent of the grazing that leads us to the highest illumination is described by the Lord in the *Bhagavad Gita*. (10:9-11):

With their thought on Me, with their life absorbed in Me, instructing each other and ever speaking of Me, they are content and delighted.

To these ever devout, worshipping Me with love, I give that devotion of knowledge by which they come to Me.

Out of mere compassion for them, I, abiding in their Self, destroy the darkness born of ignorance by the luminous lamp of wisdom.

It was said earlier that religions are means to an end that transcends religion. They are aids to inner illumination. When illumination dawns, we realize that our true nature is in essence identical with God, the Absolute, Brahman. The purpose of religion is to remove the covering from our eyes so that we may see directly and experience for ourselves the spiritual truth that is the source of all religion. 'Blessed are the pure in heart for they shall see God.' (*Matthew*, 5:8)

To take an image from the Gospels, the spiritual teachings are like the curative paste that Jesus prepared and applied to the eyes of the blind beggar. Once the man's sight was restored, the paste had served its purpose. In the spiritual Yoga the teacher is compared to someone who treats defective eyes in order to restore a person to normal sight. The Guru is revered as one, who, with the collyrium of knowledge of truth, removes, as it were, the eye disease of those blinded by spiritual ignorance.

TRUE CHRISTIANITY AND YOGA

In both Christianity and Yoga this awakening concerns what we know ourselves to be. If we learn to think
of ourselves as Atman, not the body, not the mind, it is
more than an intellectual idea. For this idea gives indirect knowledge of our reality and undermines our false
identification with the mental world. The conviction: 'In
my true nature, I am Atman', makes possible the
realization: 'I am ever liberated.' In the words of Shri
Shankara, from his *Thousand Teachings* (10:3):

> I am without a second, unborn, deathless, not subject to
> old age, immortal, self-luminous, omnipresent, not a
> cause, not an effect, completely without taint, ever one,
> perfectly satisfied, liberated.

The way to this realization is indicated by Meister
Eckhart, a knower of truth from the Christian tradition,
whose teachings mirror those of Adhyatma Yoga.

> The seed of God is in us. Given an intelligent farmer
> and a diligent fieldhand, it will thrive and grow up to
> God, whose seed it is and, accordingly, its fruit will be
> God-nature. Pear seeds grow into pear trees; nut seeds
> into nut trees; and God-seed into God!

13

FROM EGOISM TO DIVINITY

TO THOSE whose spiritual eyes are open, there is the realization that one supreme power underlies this world of appearances, and it is the ultimate source of all the laws that hold our universe together. The word 'universe' implies a single complete system embracing all space and time, matter and energy. But when we enter the world of man, there is a change of perspective. In our all-too-human affairs, the underlying unity is forgotten, and we focus on establishing our particular stake in the universe, often clashing with others in the process. Nonetheless, the hidden harmony is always there and can be realized as the only true experience. The knowers of ultimate truth have awakened to this underlying spiritual unity and this experience brings inexpressible peace and complete fulfilment.

Our longing for peace and fulfilment becomes the motive power for our spiritual quest, because, after repeated experiences and disappointments in the world, we are compelled to look within, and it is in our own being that the great discovery is made through acquiring the deepest kind of self-knowledge. Yet this self-knowledge ultimately transcends what is personal and limited, just as space transcends all boundaries and enclosures. Spiritual self-knowledge confirms our intrinsic identity with that supreme power which underlies all multiplicity. The realization is: 'One power supreme is the only one Self in each and all, and That am I.'

These are the words of Swami Rama Tirtha, a knower of truth who taught the spiritual Yoga in the early years of the last century. He was a universalist, and recognised that the same non-dual truth is the essential teaching of all religions.

On one occasion, Rama Tirtha had some guests who followed the Muslim religion. His guests found it difficult to grasp the teaching that the innermost Self of man is identical with the supreme spirit that rules the entire universe of appearances. We may share their perplexity, because the doctrine is a very subtle one. But in his explanation, Rama Tirtha shows that this view is implicit in all religions that teach the omnipotence and omnipresence of God, for God's dwelling within us as our essence and true Self follows logically from this teaching. Here is part of their interchange.

Question: You say that man is God. Is it at all possible?
Answer: Why man alone? All that we see, feel or imagine is nothing but God.
Question: But how is that possible?

Rama Tirtha then reminded his guests of the saying in their own holy book: 'God is nearer to you than the jugular vein.' This statement of the immediacy of God has to be taken as applying to everyone and everything.

'Therefore, according to your own Quran, you have to see God in everything, because He is in everything.'

He once again reminded his guests of the teaching that runs all through their holy book: that God is limitless, present everywhere and all-powerful. Such a view of God must abolish any idea that He is fundamentally separate from man. 'He is therefore not at all separate from you. As such He is one with you. And when He is one with you in entirety, where is the difference between you and God?'

This characteristic teaching of the spiritual Yoga is not just a religious point of view, a matter of faith. It is subject to confirmation in our own experience. It is revealed in Self-knowledge. Adhyatma Yoga is a walkable and well-signposted path that leads to this realization.

But if the Self of man is identical with God, which self are we talking about? It is surely something very deep. What is meant is that the spirit of man is the true Self, and *that* is identical with God. To realize this truth, Swami Rama told his guests, 'Change your worldliness to godliness. It means that you should sublimate your selfishness into the selflessness of Godhood.' Elsewhere he said: 'The spirit of religion is essentially a change of heart. It is to replace egoism by divinity.'

In order to effect this change of heart, we do not have to do anything complicated. The solution to our spiritual problem is close at hand. The doctrine of the

Upanishads is that the divinity, the Godhead, already underlies human egoism as its true nature. Our higher path is to learn how to transcend selfish egoism—this preoccupation with our individuality—in order to realize the glory and freedom of the true Self that underlies it. All spiritual practices are devised in order to help us effect this transcendence—to forget our limited self and lose ourselves in the beauty, truth and purity of the infinite Self.

Our sense of 'I' may at present appear to be stubbornly entangled in our individual body and mind, like a graceful kite that has got itself caught in the branches of a tree. The purpose of the kite is to sail free in the sunlit air, and our ultimate purpose as human beings is to realize the freedom and infinitude of the Self. In practice, we feel a keen sense of identity with our passing vehicles, the body and the mind, which seem to keep us entangled in this world of limited experiences. But there are ways and means of extricating ourselves from this false and restrictive sense of identity, and of withdrawing our identity back into its true base, the infinite spirit, the innermost Self, which is one with the divine ground of all being and intelligence, the supreme reality, God.

The ego is what we refer to when we use the word 'I'. When we speak of egoism, it can mean something excessive, as when a person not only thinks about himself all the time, but tends to believe he is the main subject of everyone else's thoughts and conversation. But more simply and universally, egoism is the natural sense of identification with an individual body and mind. The more thoughtful we become about life, the more we are likely to realize that this identity is a state of bondage and restriction. Not only do we find ourselves imprisoned in something that is bound to perish one day. If we think we are only the body and mind, we are certainly vulnerable to 'the heartache and the thousand natural shocks that flesh is heir to', to quote the words of Hamlet.

But we may draw comfort from the spiritual philosophy of Yoga. This philosophy shows clearly how our sense of identification with the body, mind, intellect and individualised ego, is a false identification. It is an illusory connection, set up by wrong knowledge. And this connection is dissolved by right knowledge—the realization of the essential truth that our real Self is in essence identical with God. On the realization of this truth, any real connection of the infinite Self with the limited and perishable body is seen to be impossible. It is the light of spiritual knowledge that will dispel all our limited notions of selfhood, and effect the realization of our natural state, perfect freedom, peace, fulfilment and fearlessness.

We have the opportunity to bring about within ourselves a change of heart, replacing egoism by divinity, and that divinity lies behind the ego. Divinity

177

unrealized is the real cause of the ego's restlessness and also of its pretensions. The ego knows that there is greatness within it, but sources it in the wrong place. The greatness belongs to the underlying spirit, which enlivens all egos, and is one in all. Through egoism we limit ourselves, and through realizing our divinity we free ourselves from all bondage.

This spiritual principle is expressed in a poem by Swami Rama Tirtha called 'The Fruits of Renunciation':

When I renounced enjoyment of the flowers
for my personal pleasure,
The whole earth became my garden.
When I renounced joy in taste,
The whole world became a delicacy.
When the eyes gave up yearning for beauty,
Beauty displayed herself before me.
When I ceased to desire the delights of the open air,
The morning breeze became my own.
When I gave up the desire for listening,
All music and song became mine.
When dreams of personal advantage left me,
I myself became all beautiful dreams.
Strange, I own nothing at all,
I lay no claim to body or personality.
If I have eyes, hands and feet,
They belong to everyone;
Yet the whole world has become my own.

Therefore our self-centredness is entirely natural and for a very good reason. It turns out to be an indirect indicator of our divinity. The ego, deep down, will always crave significance, for the simple reason that in its spiritual nucleus, it is infinitely significant, itself being all. But in this spiritual realization, the limited phase of the ego is transcended. Then, there can be no return to the constricted idea that our real being, our true Self or I, is imprisoned in a perishable body and mind.

Similarly we are right to love ourselves the most, because our innermost Self, our true centre, is the home of beauty, harmony and peace, and is lovable above all else. But to get this self-love right, we have to see through the phase of our egoity which is wrapped up in the body and the mind. To penetrate our own essence is to realize that our innermost Self is all-in-all, one in all, the supreme spirit itself.

Emanating from this highest truth, the meditation texts of Adhyatma Yoga are often expressed in the first person, 'I'.

OM I am love. I am the ocean of bliss and light, absolutely self-sufficient and self-illumined. OM

OM I am taintless, immovable, infinite, pure, free from old age and death. I am not the body, which is ever changing and unreal. OM

Direct Experience of Reality, verse 28.

179

With such texts, the ego sings the song of its true nature. Its limited circle widens and dissolves, and merges with the infinite truth that underlies it.

This notion of 'I', which is first associated with egoity and personal identity, is the precious clue to the divinity that is its source. By knowing the true nature of the Self, one knows all. We discover our Godhead, our divine nature, through centring our attention on this sense of 'I' within us, and withdrawing more deeply into it, with the help of a holy text, forgetting all limited ideas of who or what we are. What remains is pure existence, consciousness and bliss. In the words of Swami Rama Tirtha:

Get rid of this false notion. Realize your true Self to be the All. Rise above selfish egoism and you are happy this moment, one with the whole universe. You have no right to claim this mind or intellect to yourself and deny everything else. The wide world, the whole universe, is yours. Realize that. Just regain your birthright, and all anxiety and misery ceases.

This is a challenging course, because of our rooted habits and ways of thought. But we can cultivate new ways of thought, response and action, that will transform our life through awakening our power of spiritual intuition. The divine Self, the supreme spirit, is present in all experience. Our powers of action and knowledge have their source and origin in the spirit, and not in our physical life. The spirit sustains the world, as its inner ruler. This is the teaching of the Upanishads—that the supreme spirit does not rule the world from above, but from within, just as the thread holds together the necklace. One of the names for God in the Upanishads is 'thread' or *sutra*, and Rama Tirtha calls this thread 'the subtle principle, truth'.

If God is ever present, we can make the transition from egoism to the ever-present divinity at any point in our daily life. This is the secret of the Yoga of action. The life of work, whether in company with others or alone, is a heaven-sent opportunity to dissolve the ego and realize Godhead. But the secret is to forget oneself in the work, to lose oneself in it, so that all selfish motivation and anxious concern for appreciation or reward, are expelled from our consciousness.

This is not the way of the world. But we are seeking something higher than the transient worldly gains and, as we shall find, if we can work in this spirit, the best possible work will always be done through us, and our daily bread will not fail us. We will not miss out on the little gains the world can offer, but we *will* miss out on the anxiety, the stress, the tension, the feverish concern with what people are thinking about us, that so often accompanies and mars our work in the world. The real work is not that which is done when all the time we are wishing we were somewhere else, or hanging on the appreciation of others. The real work is performed with happy absorption in the work for its own sake because it ought to be done, because the divine life has connected us with this particular type of labour, and for the time being this is what we are meant to be doing.

The whole point of working in this way is that our work itself will throw us, so to say, into a higher state of consciousness. How is this so? Behind the curtain of egoity lies the infinitude and freedom of divinity. If we can forget our individuality in work, of whatever kind, we can rise above this ego idea, and rest our consciousness in the divine.

It is true that many people who know nothing about this higher Yoga work with utter absorption and self-forgetfulness while the work is going on. Their minds are in a condition similar to the *ekagrata*—one-pointedness—cultivated by the yogis, and during this time of focused attention, there is tranquil joy. The real source of such joy is the divine region that underlies the ego, and which is revealed, so to say, when the ego is forgotten. But in these worldly instances, the workers afterwards feel connected with the results of their work, and suffer or enjoy accordingly. Thus they remain in the bondage of individuality.

In Yoga we are taught to work in this self-forgetting way *consciously* by offering our actions and their results to that divine power that is all-pervasive. In this way, the actions become sanctified for their own sake, and we transcend identification with them and their outcome.

When we offer our work to the supreme power, the divinity, the inner ruler, that subtle principle truth on which all experience is threaded, we enjoy great relief. The negative trends of our personality are forgotten and fall away. In other words, our inner being is purified. And the purer our mind, the more we will become aware of the divinity behind the limited ego.

The idea is not to renounce work, but to renounce the selfish undercurrent of thoughts, distractions, resentments and temptations that so often accompany work and reduce its effectiveness. This is summed up in Krishna's advice to Arjuna in the *Bhagavad Gita*:

Renouncing all action in Me (the Divine), with thy thought resting on the Self, being free from hope, free from selfishness, devoid of fever, do thou fight (i.e. work). (3:30)

In order to work in this way, we need to develop a certain degree of self-awareness and to sharpen our understanding of what our mind is doing at any given moment. This kind of alertness is greatly helped by daily practice of meditation. For in meditation, we not only try to calm and spiritualize our mind. We also get to know something of the mind's way of functioning. We gain in alertness and self-knowledge, and this alertness will naturally feed into our life of action. For example, we will become more aware of our reactions, and then we can quickly intervene and correct matters by replacing tension or anger with equanimity, if necessary.

As a complementary practice, Swami Rama Tirtha recommends taking a timely pause during our life of action to affirm our higher nature and forget the body and mind. In an essay entitled 'Rest', he writes:

> While at work, between whiles, devote a spare interval of a moment or so to the thought that there is but one reality, God, thy Self. As to the body, etc., you never had anything to do with it. You are simply a witness, you have nothing to do with the consequences or the result. Thus contemplating, you may close your eyes, relax your muscles and lay the body perfectly at ease, unburdening yourself of all thought. The more you succeed in taking off the burden of thought from your shoulders, the stronger you will feel.

The general principle is clear, even if we may need to adjust some of the details to suit our own circumstances. There are always such intervals in a normal working day, however brief. Many people at work arrange for themselves deliberate times to take a snack. We also need spiritual nourishment, so we may compare our efforts to rest our mind and focus on the one reality, to taking a spiritual snack of wholesome food that will do us great good on every occasion.

These are short but effective practices through which we can learn to rise above the ego even in the midst of daily life. Here is another such practice:

OM. For one minute, cast overboard all desire; chant OM; no attachment, no repulsion, perfect poise, and there your whole being is Light personified. OM

Alternatively, we may spend our minute focusing on the central thought: 'OM. I am Light. OM.'

The feeling of self-love is natural and can never be eradicated because it is based on the deeper truth that our inmost Self—the divinity behind the egoity—is the home of all beauty, bliss, peace and delight. While we are unenlightened about our deeper spiritual Self, our self-love gets hijacked and confined within our individual body and mind, because that is what we think our self to be. Wherever we feel self-hood or identity, there our love flows. When a mother loves her baby, it is natural, because it springs from her own being and she has self-feeling for it.

The logic of this is that as our self-feeling widens, so does our love. And when our sense of Self is firmly planted in the divinity underlying our egoism, we naturally love all, because we realize the infinitude of our being and our oneness with all. If we can love our little self so faithfully, we can surely love our Self in its realized and expanded nature as one with the Self of the universe.

In fact, we do not love the Self. We love *as* the Self, because the Self is Love itself. In this way, Adhyatma Yoga leads us to a new way of feeling as well as of acting. If we cannot immediately feel our oneness with all, at least we can turn our thoughts in that direction. This has to be done consciously through meditation on the underlying unity of all, on the sanctity of all life, by virtue of that divine *sutra* or thread running through it as the vital factor.

At the same time, our universal vision must be a sympathetic one, seeing the good in things and ignoring what we think are the defects. Love unites, but criticism divides. The critical spirit that fixes on the faults in our fellow men, darkens our own mind and keeps us in duality and difference. It is never relieved by expression. One of Swami Rama Tirtha's mottoes is this: 'If you know anything unworthy of a friend, forget it. If you know anything pleasant about the person, tell it.' Instead of focusing on the faults of our friend or acquaintance, the best criticism is to make people feel from within what you wish to make them realize from without.

It means replacing antagonism with peace and goodwill, and seeing people differently. Instead of 'demonising' individuals or groups, we think: How would I like them to be? What is the ideal? And for a spiritual person, the ideal is summed up in the sentence

186

from the *Isha Upanishad*: 'Cover all with God'. In covering all with God, we are covering all with what they really are in essence. This principle, applied not just to others but to ourselves, is the real way to render spiritual service.

Our true nature is the eternal non-dual reality. Any other conception of human nature is due to ignorance—confounding our true being with the individualised body and mind. This notion deludes us like a hypnotic trance, and is upheld by wrong self-suggestions. The spiritual practices are undertaken to dehypnotize us and enlighten us with self-suggestions based on the highest truth. These true suggestions enable us to extricate ourselves from this wrong identification, and to realize our self-hood as the divinity which is the true source of our self-love.

The central method to effect this realization is that of self-affirmation of a spiritual kind. The divine Self is our true being, and the spiritual affirmations express what we actually are on the deepest level, the eternal ground of being.

When we want to awaken someone who is asleep, the best way is to call their name. The name, above all other words and notions, has the power to penetrate the inner darkness of sleep and cause an awakening stir of recognition. In the same way, the spiritual affirmations, which join this little word 'I' with the divine, rouse, as it were, the sleeping godhead within us. Here is one such affirmation:

OM
I AM THE SUN THAT NEVER SETS.
I AM IMMORTAL, ALL-PERVASIVE AND BLISS.
OM

14

SELF IS THE GREATEST GAIN

The sages hold that there is no greater gain than the gain of Atman, one's own higher Self. With a view to this gain, the sage adores his own Self, the Supreme Lord.

Sureshvara's *Manasollasa*, 1.2

LET US LOOK a little more deeply at the philosophy that underlies the Adhyatma Yoga. Its concern is with self-knowledge, not in the sense of knowing what kind of a personality we are, but with the deeper aim of realizing the ultimate light and support of our nature. The yogic insight is that each and every human being is in essence divine. This refers to our spiritual nature, transcending our personality and our limited individuality. To know it, to realize it, leads to perfect peace and fulfilment.

If we find ourselves drawn to this ideal of self-transcendence, we will appreciate the verses of a short, great Vedanta classic called the *Avadhut Gita*, for their sole aim and purpose is to aid our spiritual awakening. Each verse of the *Avadhut Gita* reminds us of our own intrinsic godhead, and recalls our mind to its divine source, through the revelation that our true nature is infinite. Any other picture of ourselves is a product of wrong knowledge, faulty understanding.

Our true being is the underlying reality of all, transcending all forms, and is perfection itself:

I alone am, ever free from all taint. The world exists within me like a mirage. To whom shall I bow? (1:3)*

It is the ultimate statement of our true nature, the realization that there is only the Self, partless, un-divided, and I am That. The realization that there is nothing over and above the Self leads logically to the following declaration:

How can I salute the Self, which is indestructible, which is all bliss, which in itself and by itself pervades everything, and which is inseparable from itself? (1:2)

Man is the starting point, because the divine nature has to be uncovered in our own being as its very nucleus. But once the light of wisdom is uncovered, even such notions as manhood, humanity, other people, the outer world—all these notions are transcended in the completely unified and fulfilled experience known as non-duality.

Such statements of the illumined sages, if we are ready to welcome them and give them our attention, will serve as a powerful antidote to the outer suggestions that throw our mind into the whirlpools of desires,

* The numbering is based on Hari Prasad Shastri's translation of the *Avadhut Gita*, published by Shanti Sadan.

worries and moods. Above all, these pointers to transcendent truth awaken that intuitive knowledge of our fundamental divinity, freedom and infinity—an intuition that may be in hibernation at the moment, but will one day emerge as the ultimate fact of our nature. This spiritual vision is universal and it applies to everyone:

> Know the Self to be infinite consciousness, self-evident, beyond destruction, enlightening all bodies equally, ever shining. In It is neither day nor night. (1:11)

Direct teachings like these assume a thorough preparation on the part of the enquirer. This preparation involves fostering an inner atmosphere of peace and harmlessness, and maturing our capacity to focus the mind on symbols of the deeper reality. This inner application makes us sensitive to the living power of the spiritual statements, which then become a source of upliftment. If we feel attracted to these teachings and recognise something valuable in them, it is the result— or reward—of a certain evolution that has already taken place within us. There has been a clearing in the mind, a decrease of narrow self-interest, releasing a natural attraction for teachings that proclaim the unity of the Self with God. And this attraction is itself made possible by the grace of God.

By the grace of God, some are inspired with a disposition to non-duality (unity of the Self with God), which relieves them of the great fear (of death). (1:1)

This means a highly favourable change has come about within us. We have turned in the right direction towards the source of wisdom—within. By 'God' is meant the divine presence that is the innermost essence of our own consciousness. That 'grace' is essentially a release or revelation that has its source in our own higher nature. But this grace or inner light is only revealed if we ourselves have created the inner conditions suitable to its revelation. If we have created a bent of mind based on peace, universal goodwill and a deep desire for inner freedom, we have, by this very tendency, begun to purify our vision. A kind of vacuum is created, and this vacuum is filled by the spiritual influence that emanates from the depths of our own soul. This influence is called grace. Through this grace arises the pure desire for complete spiritual freedom, for the unity of the Self with God.

To bring out our highest spiritual potentialities, we need to feel we are moving towards a clear goal, a definite end-point. The climax of human evolution is God-realization or Self-realization. To be conscious of this goal is fundamental to progress in Yoga. We gain spiritual light and power by opening our mind to the sayings of those who have reached the goal. What they express is impersonal and spontaneous, and points to an enlightened experience beyond the range of the human intellect.

> Neither can it be said 'It is' nor 'It is not.' What a great mystery! (1:4)

Words can only be pointers or clues. But they are vital clues. They stimulate our deeper intuition. They direct us to a realm of freedom and illumination that is close at hand. For the goal turns out to be the Self of the seeker. Right now, always, it is identical with the supreme power that religions call God or truth, and that in Yoga is called Brahman, meaning the Absolute, the ultimate reality. The goal is never distant or remote. It is 'ever-attained'.

This fact—that our goal is ever attained—has to be realized, not produced or acquired. While we are preparing for this awakening, the concept of a goal or peak to work towards is meaningful and necessary. It encourages us to make the right inner adjustments. But this goal orientation is only sustainable up to a certain point. It merges into self-identification through affirmation. When the error of non-realization is cancelled, one's Self is realized as the only reality.

> That God, who is the Self in all, impersonal and changeless, like unto space, by nature purity itself, verily, verily, that am I. (1:6)

Speaking metaphorically, this realization is the peak

of the mountain of Yoga. To reach this peak is the reason for taking up the spiritual Yoga. Utterances or verses proclaiming the ultimate truth, point to a consummation of experience. They give us an idea of the summit. This view of the summit, however hazy or distant, is essential if we are to sustain our sense of direction. It is important to keep in our mind's eye our ultimate goal of self-realization if we are to awaken the highest wisdom within ourselves. This summit cannot be reached by a sudden sprint, or a daring rope-swing across a perilous chasm. There is only one way to climb a mountain, and it is step by step. One false step, one self-willed departure from the traditional path, can result in a slip or mishap that might hinder our ability for further advance. The highest truth, which is the very ground of our being, is approached gradually, through stages of the refinement of our understanding.

> Atman (our spiritual Self), of which the high yogis speak, most subtle, beyond perception, without attributes, must be realized step by step, and not by sudden violence. (2:12)

The training in Yoga is to tranquillize and purify our mind and emotions, and to dissolve the sense of egoism, so that our intuition of the immortality and infinitude of our real Self becomes a matter of direct experience. When this realization dawns, the self-reference indicated by the word 'I' transcends both the finite personality and the world of time and space. It refers to ultimate reality.

> I am without beginning and without end. Never was I bound. By nature pure, taintless is my Self. This I know for certain. (1:38)

> The state of eternal peace, the higher transcendental truth, space-like, am I. (3:14)

A thing may be very near, it may be within or around us, but it may be too subtle for us to see or to understand. We naturally ask: 'How can one affirm the infinitude of one's true nature, when it is obvious that we are limited, and that we encounter restrictions and obstacles all through life?' The answer is that we are not just body and mind, but body, mind and spirit. And just as the mind is a subtler principle than the body, so too the spirit is subtlest of all and completely transcends both body and mind.

We know the mind is subtler than the body. Our thoughts can fly with the angels, so to say, though the body be in chains. Our intellect, through its subtlety, can fathom the laws of nature. But the mind itself shares the inner realm with an altogether more subtle and superior principle. This is the spirit, transcending all mental activity. It is like a steady, fundamental light that reveals all experience, both mental and physical. This is our true Self, the real nature of our innermost consciousness, and it is infinite and non-dual.

Ultimate fulfilment is achieved when we recognise basic identity with this dimension of our being. At this level, our nature is free from all limitations and universal.

One simile, given for our reflection, is that of space—vast, boundless, all-pervasive and subtle. 'Space-like am I'. Space is a valuable 'image'. Like the spiritual reality, it is ever-present, undivided and untouched by objects and events. Itself motionless, without space there could be no movement at all for anything. Itself a perfect and continuous unity, it is the necessary stage for all multiplicity. Space is a subtle conception. A car occupies a segment of space, but when it drives off, it does not take the space with it. Space remains undisturbed, constant and complete, whatever happens to the things that appear within it. Yet we need to remember that space is only a simile for the infinite nature of our true Self. The Self is not space, but space-like. The Avadhut sings: 'More subtle than space itself am I.' The space simile gives us an idea of the unbroken and unstained freedom of enlightenment.

All ideas are destined to dissolve under the light of direct experience of reality.

When as a pilgrim I began to journey towards Thee, then all my little notions of the all-pervasiveness of Atman died. (7:1)

One has to form an idea of the goal and to develop a

consciousness of the goal, with the help of these holy texts. But we need to stay open-minded, and be receptive to new insights that will enhance our present understanding with something deeper and closer to the truth.

The word *avadhut* comes from a Sanskrit root that means 'to shake off'. It has an inner meaning. Our true nature is already divine. But this state of ever-achieved liberation and perfection has become as if clouded over by the idea that we are separate individuals identified with a particular body and mind. What is necessary is to banish this cloud—to shake it off by realizing its unreality from the standpoint of ultimate truth. The antidote to this false identification is to affirm our essential identity with our real Self, the conscious light, the underlying reality. This is to sift the not-self from the Self. This process paves the way to the highest knowledge.

> Know all forms, physical and subtle, as illusion. The reality underlying them is eternal. By living this truth, one passes beyond birth and death. (1:21)

The supreme positivity—eternal reality—is approached through apparent negation: not this, not this. The process of negation is achieved through the constant practice of stilling the mind and charging it with the affirmation of our intrinsic identity with the Absolute. It is by soaking the mind in these great affirmations of our identity with absolute truth, that we awaken to the realization of the reality behind the words.

To affirm 'I am the Absolute' does not add a new quality to the I. It negates the notion that I am anything other than the Absolute. The Avadhut sings:

I am neither bound nor free. I am not separate from Brahman. (1:43)

What emerges from all this is that we have a choice in what we decide to be identified with. We can insist on the authority and validity of our finite personality, which is changing all the time and which, sooner or later, will perish. Or we can learn to take our stand on, and realize, our spiritual nature, which is infinite and immortal. In affirming this, we are not saying that our limited personality is divine. We are saying that our limited personality has no independent reality and only the universal divine essence truly *is.* That am I. Our true nature transcends the temporary enclosures of our body, mind and personality, and has a glory and majesty that defies all description:

This Consciousness Absolute words cannot describe. The mind is lost in its majesty. How can I describe to thee this eternal? I can but say that this immortality-giving knowledge, space-like, am I. (3:11)

SHANTI SADAN PUBLICATIONS

*Vedanta classics in English translation
mentioned in this book*

ASHTAVAKRA GITA

AVADHUT GITA

CREST-JEWEL OF WISDOM
Viveka-Chudamani

DIRECT EXPERIENCE OF REALITY
Aparokshanubhuti

THOUSAND TEACHINGS OF SHANKARA
Upadesha-Sahasri

TRIUMPH OF A HERO
Vira Vijaya

UNDERSTANDING 'THAT THOU ART'
Vakya Vritti

*   *   *

SELF-KNOWLEDGE Yoga Quarterly
devoted to spiritual thought and practice

*   *   *

For illustrated book catalogue contact:

Shanti Sadan, 29 Chepstow Villas, London W11 3DR

www.shantisadan.org